PERSONAL
J O B
POWER

Discover your own
power style for
work satisfaction
and success

**Clay Carr
and Valorie Beer**

DEDICATION

Clay Carr did not live to see this book completed. He once wrote to me that he was worried that no teacher had come for him. Perhaps he didn't realize that Sages don't need teachers; they are the teachers. And he came for me.

VB

Visit Peterson's at http://www.petersons.com

Peterson's Career Focus Books: Helping people make successful job choices, maximize career potential, and stay competitive in today's workplace

Library of Congress Cataloging-in-Publication Data

Beer, Valorie.
    Personal job power :   discover your own power style for work
satisfaction and success / by Valorie Beer & Clay Carr.
        p.   cm.
    Includes bibliographical references and index.
    ISBN 1-56079-599-9
    1. Career development.   2. Self-actualization (Psychology)
I. Carr, Clay, 1934—   . II. Title.
HF5381.B3552   1996
650.14—dc20   96-31263
                                                         CIP

Editorial direction by Carol Hupping   Creative direction by Linda Huber
Production supervision by Bernadette Boylan   Interior design by Cynthia Boone
Composition by The Clarinda Company

CONTENTS

ACKNOWLEDGMENTS

This book grew out of our own experiences as managers and employees in a variety of organizations. Invaluable to us were our conversations with innumerable colleagues who helped to sharpen the book's focus. We'd particularly like to thank the board and membership of the International Society for Performance Improvement (ISPI), whose members supported us with their insights and enthusiasm, and whose conferences and meetings provided us with those rare opportunities to actually see each other.

Our families gave us the space to sit and think (or to type furiously in a fit of creative energy). They were always there with good ideas and a caring "How's the book coming?" Our love and thanks to Gayle, Lisa, Heather, Brian, Suzanne, Houston, Dick, Raye, and Bonnijill.

Mike Snell, our agent, stayed with us during the months in which we tried to figure out both what we wanted to write and how to make it marketable. And finally, our deepest appreciation to Carol Hupping, our editor at Peterson's. Her competence as an editor and her compassion and encouragement as a human being were a great support, especially to Valorie after Clay's passing. She caught our vision and helped us bring it to fruition.

THE SEARCH FOR REAL POWER IN THE WORKPLACE

E *mpowerment:* As an organizational and management development strategy, it's high on the buzzword list, yet its success in the workplace has been mixed. If you've been through an "empowerment" program, you may feel that you have more control over your work life. Or you may feel that you've just been used for someone else's purposes, that you've been "given" power so that you'll do more of what the organization wants. This is especially true if you've been *told* that now you have more power, yet everything in the organization seems to go on as before.

If you're a manager in such an organization, it may seem that everyone else is being given power at your expense. If you're an employee, you may find that you're caught in the old "responsibility without authority" trap; that is, you've been given the power to produce the same thing faster or even at a higher quality level, without the authority to make decisions about strategies, processes, or the products themselves. In either case, you're not alone; thousands, probably

1

millions, of workers and managers across the U.S. have mixed feelings about and mixed experiences with "empowerment."

This book is not about empowerment in the sense of giving power to others or expecting them to give it to you. Rather, it is about identifying and developing the power that is already within you so that you can do rewarding work without depending on a *particular* place, organization, manager, or set of colleagues for the impetus to do that work. This doesn't mean that you'll be able to work with complete independence; truly powerful people value the relationships in which they use and renew their power. What it does mean is that finding your power within will give you more stability in a turbulent job market because you will have identified how you want to behave (rather than how you want to be controlled) in your job. That is, using your own personal power will help you to be internally independent from the expectations and "shoulds" of others (including your own inner voice), without cutting yourself off from stimulating and nurturing workplace relationships.

You are poised to take maximum advantage of an examination of your personal job power if you:

- find yourself trying to exercise your own personal power in a new or uncertain work environment where your survival and livelihood depend on maximizing your innate capacity to do good work
- feel stuck because your innate capacities have been consistently ignored or even punished, and you want to find ways to gain self-assurance about your value as a workplace contributor
- are worried about what the organization is going to do with you in the next round of layoffs, downsizings, redeployments, and "voluntary" retirements
- find that others' efforts to "give" you power just make you cynical and distrustful (even if those efforts are sincere, have the backing of top management, etc.)

- are contemplating a career change, especially one that takes you from a more structured, controlling environment to one that is less so (if you're planning to join a consultancy, for example, or start your own business)
- want to recognize and enhance your own personal power to make your workplace a better place, your job a better job, and your work life more satisfying and productive

This book is not just for "managers," "employees," "supervisors," or "executives." It is for anyone in an organization who wants to develop his or her own power and find his or her own innate worth rather than depend on others to bestow power or a sense of worth upon them.

However, developing your own job power is not as simple as just deciding to do it. There are several conflicting trends in today's work environment, such as empowerment and downsizing, that will pull you in different directions. The key point to keep in mind is that these programs usually are imposed on you or given to you, whereas this book focuses on selecting the "program" for finding and developing your own power within you. Personal power is not:

- an organizational program
- something handed to employees by managers
- conversely, something demanded from management by employees
- the replacement of openly authoritarian control processes with more indirect and manipulative ones
- something that one person can give to or take from another

Think of power as a state of being and as something that only you can do for yourself, instead of as some *thing* that you take from or give to others. Such a view makes personal power volitional. It's under your control. And while you can't "empower" anyone else, you can act effectively by using your own power to create an environment that favors (or at least doesn't hinder) both you and others in the development and exercise of true personal power. This means that job power doesn't require a hierarchy, and it works whether you are a "manager" or an "employee." In fact, those terms become less steeped in traditional meaning, since in an organization made up of powerful individuals, differences between managers and employees become less rigid.

So why isn't the power that you may get from management or from your organization enough? Why is developing and skillfully using your own personal power so important to doing the work you want to do and deriving satisfaction from it? The answer lies in the changes that are taking place in the workplace itself.

LIVING IN A WORLD WITHOUT CAREERS

"Career" doesn't mean what it used to. No manager or worker can count on stable, predictable, lifelong employment (in other words, a career) in today's workplaces. *Fortune* magazine, for example, compared work today not to marriage but to a series of brief affairs (June 13, 1994). As such, work seems to become a game played in a highly uncertain environment in which you sell your skills to the highest bidder, and your employer helps to develop you just enough to make you productive.

Neither you nor your organization may have heart and soul in the partnership; at any time, you can take your intellectual capital and invest it somewhere else, or the organization can decide that it doesn't need your talents. In such circumstances, are companies seriously going to encourage managers and employees to look out for their personal interests, even if it means that they'll leave the company at a critical time? We think not. On the other hand, if companies assume the right to let go of even their best and brightest members whose skills are no longer needed, people (such as you) who work in those organizations must seize the right to manage their own destinies, whether this suits the company or not. In short, the traditional underpinnings of a stable work relationship—trust and loyalty—have changed dramatically, and that in turn changes the definition of what it means to have power in the workplace and who has that power.

THE LIMITS OF TRUST AND LOYALTY

The American workforce is worn out by reengineering and downsizing. You may have heard in your workplace that "this time we've cut to the muscle and bone" or "all of the good people are leaving." In a series of articles focusing on management, *The Economist* made the following observation; it goes right to the heart of this struggle for power and control in the workplace:

> *In a world in which the life expectancy of the average Fortune 500 company is 40 years (and shrinking), and in which giants such as AT&T celebrate a new year by sacking 40,000 people, employees might find a better focus than companies for their feelings of loyalty.* (January 6, 1996, p. 49)

In short, neither your place in the workplace nor your company's hold on you is guaranteed. Perhaps you've felt this directly already if you've been laid off or redeployed or if you've taken your talents to several workplaces in the past few years. The traditional equation in which you traded your power and your creativity for security and a paycheck is gone, for both you and the organizations that hire you.

What to do, then? Giving up your power to an employer clearly isn't the path to job security anymore; however, most of us still need (and want) to go to workplaces to make a living and exercise our creative talents. The key is to stop expecting your workplace to give you the power to do your job and, instead, to find and develop the power you have within you so that the actual work (and not the place it's done) gets more of your energy and attention. That is, you need to look at power not as something you get but as something you already have. Let's take a look at what personal power means in the context of the work you do.

THE KEYS TO YOUR PERSONAL JOB POWER

Powerful people abound in your workplace. They're the ones who get what they want for their projects, their staffs, and themselves by speaking up and acting in other "powerful" ways. Perhaps you think, "If only I could be like them. . . ." The problem is, in this day and age it's sometimes hard to distinguish the exercise of genuine personal power from self-serving manipulation. In short, you might be hard-pressed to tell if you and other people in your organization are acting powerfully or just getting away with murder.

In this section, we'll define personal power (as distinct from empowerment) and introduce the general characteristics of that power and how you'll use it in the workplace. Despite our earlier comments on organizations that don't appreciate empowered individuals, we believe the odds are better now than they have ever been that you will find a job where you can exercise your personal power. When this happens, you will find work is far more satisfying, and you accomplish more real results, than you ever thought possible.

PERSONAL POWER DEFINED

Personal power is not just something you do, a set of skills you go out and acquire; it's something you already have. Developing that power means that you do two things:

1. You actively use your power to be what you want to be in your work. As Connors, Smith, and Hickman put it, you "abandon the

bleacher seats and take to the playing field" in terms of getting what you need from your work. (*The Oz Principle*, p. 131)

2. You are the worker you want to be, rather than the worker someone else (a parent, a manager) wants you to be or your inner voice thinks you "should" be. In other words, you find your own path despite others' demands that you take care of their lives rather than your own.

Does this mean that you become a rugged individualist, eschewing others' desires to form relationships with you? No. Developing your own personal power will actually allow you to have more authentic relationships with others, since you won't be looking to them to recharge your batteries and meet your needs. Most importantly, you won't be looking to your coworkers or manager to provide all of the development opportunities or nurturing support that you need on the job. You will discover that:

Personal job power means living daily life in the workplace in a way that enables you to make the most constructive response possible in each situation, whether or not your organization embraces "empowerment" as a management or employee development principle.

While we acknowledge that some work situations are more conducive to the exercise of personal power than others, you can put that power to work at any level of an organization. It doesn't mean you will run the show or no longer have to worry about bosses, and it doesn't mean that you have power over others or control others. As you'll see, the definition of personal power has little to do with those traditional meanings of power. And "powerful people" are suddenly much easier to distinguish from "power charlatans," who may want and need power (yours) because they can't or won't look inside themselves to find their own real power.

PERSONAL POWER CHARACTERISTICS

Ten general traits characterize people who have found and are using their personal power at work. In a theme that we'll continue in more depth later in the book, we'll contrast those characteristics with what you might see in less powerful people. Personally powerful people:

1. *Form relationships to discover and exchange ideas and to get feedback and support.*

   Powerful people spend time with their colleagues, participating fearlessly (though respectfully) in discussion and drawing energy from the ideas and feelings expressed by others.

   Power charlatans form relationships in order to get something from others, draining others' energies and then abandoning the relationship once their own needs are met.

2. *Focus on community and collaboration, rather than on hierarchy.*

   Powerful people see themselves as legitimate contributors; even if they are novices or newcomers, they find a way to be involved.

   Power charlatans need to win, need to be on top, and rank everyone in terms of being one up or one down in relation to themselves.

3. *Attend to the needs and feelings of others as well as to their own.*

   Powerful people understand the interconnection between their own and others' situations. They know that quite a bit of energy can be wasted in repressing their own needs, and that sometimes by helping others they can resolve their own questions and concerns.

   Power charlatans either believe that others' needs and feelings can't possibly be as important as their own or give away all of their power and energy to others.

4. *Listen.*

   Powerful people spend time absorbing and integrating what others are saying (verbally and otherwise), which allows them to make connected, helpful contributions.

Power charlatans believe they are the only ones who have anything important to say.

5. *Can change their perspective when new information comes along.*
   Powerful people don't mind admitting when they're wrong and like the "ah-ha!" of seeing something in a different light.
   Power charlatans want to convert you to their (right) way of thinking.

6. *Acknowledge problems and plan solutions to realistic obstacles.*
   Powerful people anticipate issues (as well as benefits) in a course of action and create contingency plans.
   Power charlatans either expect the worst (so you can never please them) or deny the obvious problems (so you can't get the resources to fix them).

7. *Focus on progress and improvement.*
   Powerful people concentrate on how to do it better next time.
   Power charlatans look for someone to blame.

8. *Find alternatives and put ideas together differently to create new possibilities.*
   Powerful people are rarely without options.
   Power charlatans see threats and constraints to what they want to do.

9. *Take time to rest and reflect on their experiences.*
   Powerful people are comfortable "doing nothing" at times so they can process the ideas and feelings they've had all day.
   Power charlatans keep themselves (and everyone else) busy so that no one will have time to look too deeply into what's going on.

10. *Tolerate considerable ambiguity as long as a general direction has been established.*

    Powerful people can wait while the situation becomes clear for everyone, and they can then see progress in a wide variety of actions.

    Power charlatans want to tell everyone where to go and how to get there.

WHAT PERSONAL JOB POWER IS NOT

From the preceding descriptions, you now have the idea that personal power at work is not what you might typically associate with "power": It's not about control, about telling others what to do, about having the answer, or about handing out rewards and blame. Beyond the personal characteristics, though, are a couple of other keys that will help you to realize (in the sense of both to "know" and to "make real") that personal power comes from within. Remember these four keys:

- **Personal job power is not a place.**
  If you are portable, you have found your power within. If you are not portable, then you still have a power umbilical cord to a particular workplace, and you're trying to get from it things that it can't provide (such as stability or self-worth).
- **Personal job power is not a title.**
  You're a powerful vice president (or clerk) because of what you brought to the job, that is, because of qualities that you had before you got your current position. You're not suddenly powerful because of your position anymore than you are suddenly powerful because you work at a particular place.
- **Personal job power can't be given or taken.**
  It arises from an individual—you—not from colleagues or managers. They can make you feel a certain way about yourself only if you give up your power to them and trust their judgments more than you trust your own.

- **Personal job power is not freedom from ever having to work again.**
  It is the freedom to think, feel, and behave in a way that will make the work you want to do more satisfying (or the work you must do less of a drain, so you can spend your creative energy elsewhere).

WHAT'S AHEAD

Given this overview of what personal job power is and what it looks like, here's what you'll find in the pages that follow. In the next chapter, you'll learn more about personal power, including twenty specific behavioral traits of the personally powerful person. And you'll begin to see the benefits and pains that you're likely to encounter on your personal power exploration.

In Chapters 3 through 10, you'll learn about eight personal power types (including some power charlatans, or "alter egos," who are adept at deceiving you into believing that they have lots of power). Each chapter starts with examples of powerful people at work. What does it look and feel like to exercise personal power in real work situations? What joys and problems are you likely to experience? Since personal job power isn't a one-size-fits-all phenomenon, it can manifest itself in several ways.

Then we'll look at the underlying principles of personal power and the choices powerful people make about themselves and their work environments. And you will see ways in which particular types of personal power can be stressful, both for you and for your organization.

Individuals whose future depends on personal power will never be quite as "secure" as those whose company is taking care of them. There is a risk that goes with personal power, a risk that you may find quite uncomfortable at first. However, since the alternative is being tossed about at the whims of a rapidly changing economy, you'll probably quickly discover that you can ride out the discomfort of looking at your job in a new way.

Organizations, for their part, will probably be even more uncomfortable with your newfound power. Those with personal power quickly recognize when personal and organizational objectives diverge, and they often choose the personal side, leaving an organization that can no longer contribute to their needs. In addition, people with personal power can be difficult to manage or work for because the traditional rewards and behaviors that kept hierarchies alive are no longer so important to them.

To help you through the transition of letting go of external power sources and finding your own within, we'll give you several lists of power characteristics, as well as some suggestions for finding and developing your own personal power. By the end of each chapter you will be able to:

- distinguish behaviors associated with real personal power from behaviors that just seem powerful because they're loud, controlling, aloof, etc.
- identify personal powerful characteristics in yourself and others
- plan ways to develop a particular type of power in your work life

In the final chapter, we'll take a look at ways to extend your personal power to institutions and relationships beyond the workplace.

In summary, this book is not about "empowerment" in the workplace. It will not tell you how to make yourself marketable or how to negotiate a better employment contract or better salary (all of which are important, too). And it certainly won't tell you how to make others more powerful. Regardless of how magnanimous that sounds, we've seen that it is not the path to a healthy work life—either for you or for others.

Our message is that empowerment isn't an organizational phenomenon but an individual one. There are no empowered organizations, only individuals acting powerfully to meet business and personal goals. Therefore, we make no attempt to provide a balanced account of the rights and obligations of workers, managers, and organizations. Instead, we'd like to help you, as a member of a workplace, to carve out the best possible work life for yourself. Although you can't make empowerment happen, you can let the power within you come to fruition, which ultimately brings more real power to you, your colleagues, and your organization.

A PERSONAL POWER PRIMER

As we saw in Chapter 1, powerful behavior is going on around you all the time, independent of, or in spite of, programs designed to "give" you more power where you work. The point throughout this book is that real power isn't an organizational or workplace phenomenon—it's an individual phenomenon. So, in this chapter we'll take a look at some of the characteristics of personal power and begin to lay the groundwork for enhancing this power within you.

But first, a word of caution: You can't learn about your own personal power from a video or a speaker or a book (not even this one) alone; in fact, you'll find that much of the process of developing your power is a process of unlearning years of thoughts, feelings, actions, and ideas about what you should do and what you should be (and the memory of being scolded when you didn't live up to those expectations). The way to really learn about your power is by acting, not in the sense of "putting on an act," but in the sense of behaving in a way that is consistent with your thoughts and feelings and a way that invites feedback from others on the effectiveness (or ineffectiveness) of your efforts.

This isn't easy. However, there's a good chance that you are wasting some energy on actions and thoughts that drain your power away and that actually make it harder for you to maintain your energy level. You also may be trying to apply your power to finding out what's wrong with other people and speculating on what they should do or how you can fix them. Both of these actions draw power, too; that is, they aren't "easy" either, they're just familiar and comfortable ways to behave.

The counterargument is that your personal power is inherent, not learned or given. You don't need to go out and get it; you already have it, and you can learn how to enhance it. One of the best ways to do this is to associate with personally powerful people and notice how they go about being themselves. You'll discover that one of the by-products of these associations is that just opening yourself up to the ideas and actions of powerful people will enhance your own power. Being around others and being aware of how they are will help you become more powerful.

In this chapter we're going to begin to describe personal power as you might see it in yourself and others. As you read the initial descriptions, you might try thinking about people in your environment who seem personally powerful. Perhaps you'll gain more insight into the source of their powers (and your own) as you read along. Later, we'll describe ways to develop your own power—so that you can become more like who you really are (and less like who you or others think you should be).

Since no one characteristic identifies someone as personally powerful, we'll start with twenty of the more visible characteristics of that power. Sometimes you can see these characteristics directly; more often, you see only their results. However, you can also feel them in yourself, and you can begin to see and enhance their effects on yourself and others.

Before we begin with the characteristics of "personal power," let's briefly review what we mean (and don't mean) by that term.

Personal Power: What It Is, What It Isn't

As you'll recall from Chapter 1, the effective exercise of true personal power may require you to redefine what you mean by "power." So you'll have a context for the personal power characteristics that follow, we'll outline the definition of personal power that we'll use as the basis for the rest of the book. Personal power is about:

- looking deeply into and understanding your own needs and motivations
- acknowledging your limits (As you develop your personal power, you may find that you have fewer limits than you thought.)
- seeking (not just accepting) additional responsibility, without the need to make yourself feel guilty about what you're not getting done
- finding meaningful ways to contribute with the talents and skills you have or can realistically develop
- freeing yourself from the shoulds in your life: what you should be doing, the person you should be, and so forth

Personal power is NOT about:
- getting other people to do what you want
- trying to change other people so that they'll fit neatly into your world
- throwing your weight around or being bossy

- living above the law
- getting your way

Even though we're going to give you a plethora of suggestions for ways to enhance your personal power, we must emphasize that:

Personal power isn't just about what you do; it's about who you are.

The fundamental question in developing your own power is: Do you know who you are, and can you act consistently with that knowledge? Let's take a look at a graphical way of answering that question by examining the Personal Power Grid.

YOUR PERSONAL POWER GRID

A colleague of ours once said he was surprised and hurt that we could "read" him so well. He said he didn't want to be that transparent in his needs and motivations, and he was quite discomfited that his true needs (which we, as his managers, were trying to fulfill) were that obvious. We (equally surprised at his reaction) replied that most people don't have much control over how well they can be "read." The only choices our colleague (and everyone else) had were either to acknowledge and act consistently with his thoughts and feelings—or not.

As the illustration here shows, the more you know about your own thoughts, feelings, needs, and motivations, and the more you act consistently with them, the more your personal power increases. Why? First, you're applying your power to yourself (which is the only place you can apply it) in the service of your own needs, rather than using your power to bend others to your will. Second, you're using your power openly; that is, you're not using it to cover up or hide from thoughts and emotions you'd rather not face.

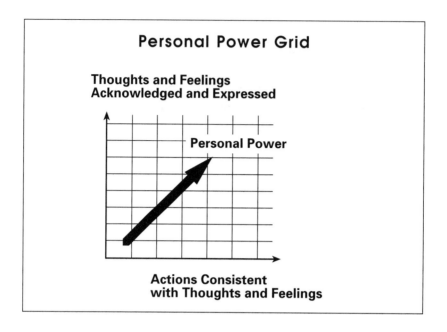

If you find you're doing well on one side of the grid but not the other, then either:

1. You're wasting your power by acting without reflecting, spending your energy without accounting for where it went (which is the problem our colleague had), or

2. Your power is stuck in idle because you're getting in touch with your thoughts and feelings without taking any action on them.

In order to realize your personal power, you need both sides of the grid: You need to be in touch and to act. This is an important point, because as we begin to describe the characteristics of personal power, you'll see that the profile of a powerful person includes thoughts, feelings, and actions that are all brought into play in a coordinated manner to make the person powerful and portable.

Let's begin by looking at some of the thoughts, feelings, and actions that characterize personally powerful people in general. In later chapters, we'll define these more specifically and make some recommendations for the enhancement of your own power.

CHARACTERISTICS OF PERSONAL POWER

While there isn't a one-size-fits-all description of people who effectively use their power, such people have made some choices and have developed some principles that enable them to act powerfully. How do these people, who are truly portable with their power and skill sets, think and feel and act? Here are twenty clues to what you might see in them:

1. *They use and renew their power in relationships.*
   These people don't define themselves as isolated individuals. You'll see them acting independently as well as *inter*dependently. That is, they think in terms of actions and solutions that benefit themselves and as many others as possible. When this isn't possible, they act in a way that minimizes damage. Or they do nothing at all. (You might say that, like medical doctors, they live by the first line of the Hippocratic oath: "Above all else, do no harm.")

2. *Although they aren't isolated, powerful people also don't feel the need to please others or to depend on others to shape their identities.*
   They don't practice gratuitous or ingratiating behaviors; however, you will see them take the needs and interests of others into account in a balanced and considerate way.

3. *They feel and acknowledge the full gamut of human emotions.*
   Powerful people feel anger, envy, despair, joy, enthusiasm, and love. They express these emotions in productive ways, so that even the most negative ones become useful. For instance, you may see them display genuine anger (without the typical component of

blame) to draw the attention of others to the seriousness of a problem they all need to address.

4. *They are constantly curious.*
   When powerful people encounter a fact, situation, or person they don't understand, they ask questions. And they never bluff when they don't know. In short, they don't seek to be experts so much as learners.

5. *They are constantly creative, but not because they need to be doing something new all the time.*
   They tend to seize opportunities, solve problems, and achieve their goals over the long haul, often because they refuse to take the easy way out or go for the quick fix. Instead, they come up with the creative solutions that go to the heart of the situation and lead to sustainable results.

6. *Although they are constantly creative, they are not constantly active.*
   As we already mentioned, people who are using their power effectively know that sometimes the most creative and compassionate response is to do nothing. They also know that rest and reflection are important for "recharging the batteries" of personal power. Even when something needs to be done, these people may wait (and wait and wait) until they believe the time is ripe for action. In short, they don't define their self-worth by how much they can get done or how busy they are.

7. *They look through problems to the opportunities hidden therein.*
   They aren't cockeyed optimists, but they do believe in making progress over time rather than dwelling on what went wrong or on what might have been.

8. *They usually say "and" instead of "but."*
   It may sound like a small behavioral quirk, but it's an indication

of how powerful people focus on opportunities. For instance, they don't say, "That's a good idea, but it raises problems." They do say, "That's a good idea, and this is how we can deal with some of the problems that might arise."

9. *They listen actively.*
    This is a key characteristic, and it raises a question: Do powerful people become powerful because they listen, or do they listen well because they are already powerful? The answer is yes to both. Powerful people listen in a way that makes those in contact with them feel they have been heard (which is tremendously empowering in itself). In addition, powerful people consciously use listening to seek feedback from others. This doesn't mean that they're overly concerned with what others think of them. It does mean that they actively seek information from others to help them evaluate and recalibrate their own goals, standards, and behavior. In addition, "listening" with more than just their ears enables powerful people to be aware of and attentive to what's going on at a variety of levels. Because they have the ability to "read" a situation on more than the verbal plane, they can perceive the real motivations and needs of others, be aware of what matters to others, and then frame problems and solutions in terms of what's important to others (as well as to themselves). They are especially adept at listening for and dealing effectively with resistance. Instead of doing more "selling" to prove their point, they'll often just ask a few questions and then listen in order to uncover and deal with the source (and not just the symptoms) of the resistance.

10. *They almost always have a deep sense of humor.*
    Powerful people take their actions and situations and goals with a lightness that's often difficult for others to understand, yet they never use humor to demean others or to separate "them" from "us."

11. *They have clear goals, and those goals are their own.*
    While they may look to others for guidance and assistance, they don't just blindly follow what others want them to do. In addition, their goals usually are stable and long-term, although how they work toward these goals often changes significantly from situation to situation. In short, powerful people can hold firm goals yet be flexible in how those goals are achieved.

12. *In addition to clear goals, powerful people have clear standards (which help them know whether they're on track as they strive to achieve those goals).*
    These standards are never simply the inherited mores of the culture, although powerful people never discard societal norms on a whim. That is, they don't flaunt their power just to prove that they're different from everyone else.

13. *They waste little time finding fault with themselves or others; instead, they spend time evaluating their actions and those of others.*
    What's the difference? Finding fault is oriented toward the past, while true evaluation looks at what was more or less effective in light of what might be done in the future. That is, when powerful people confront problems, their first thought is "What can I do to resolve the situation?" not "Who caused this, and how can I force them to accept the blame and clean up the mess they made?"

14. *While no one can live completely free of his or her past or from speculations about the future, powerful people live most of their lives in the present.*
    In particular, they are largely free of the burden of the past. They don't indulge in rethinking or feeling guilty about something that happened days or decades before, nor in thinking about how they were wrong or about how wrong was done to them. They are also free of the burden of the future, of having to cling to what they have or deny who they are in the (vain) attempt to be a different

or better person "later." (That is, powerful people know that when the "future" arrives they are likely to still feel guilty or sad or powerless unless they act now to change their perspectives.)

15. *They are open to change.*
    Powerful people are open to experimentation, to new experiences for themselves, yet they don't press others to change just to conform to their own ideas of how people should be. In addition, powerful people have a deep sense of the developing course of things. That is, they don't dissipate their energy by pushing for changes that are abstractly "right" or "good." Instead, they relate to the situation around them and act when the time is right to achieve their goals. In more common parlance, they have excellent timing.

16. *Powerful people constantly look for occasions to engage in dialogue with others.*
    In everyday discussion, individuals just toss around ideas; in dialogue, powerful people consciously attempt to use their own ideas and those of others to arrive at a better, fuller understanding of an issue. In fact, for those who are effectively using their personal power, a basic purpose of life is to engage in dialogue (which is not always verbal) and grow their own power through it.

17. *They can live with high levels of ambiguity.*
    They don't see the world in simple, black-and-white terms; they don't cling to the rule book; and they don't demand quick solutions.

18. *Powerful people are spiritual, but not necessarily in the conventional, religious sense of the word.*
    They see and live in a dimension beyond the senses, one that points to goals beyond the material, economic, and social realms. At their best, they are aware of a common humanity that tran-

scends all distinctions, and they believe that no one is really an
"other" but always a part of "us."

19. *For all these reasons—and despite what we said earlier about our
    inability to give power to others—powerful people enable others to
    be powerful.*
    How? Powerful people don't keep those around them under con-
    trol or in safe pigeonholes. Just as they rejoice in their own
    growth, they rejoice in the growth of others. They know the only
    way you can get others to act powerfully is to act that way your-
    self; they know using your own personal power calls forth and
    supports the personal power of others.

20. *Finally, and underlying all else, powerful people understand that
    they are on a journey.*
    They understand that "owning" power is not a destination. Power
    is not a place itself, nor is it associated with a place (such as where
    you work). This knowledge, above all else, makes powerful people
    portable.

THE STRAINS AND JOYS
OF PERSONAL POWER

So far we've talked about personal power as if using it will make everything turn out right. However, there are some disadvantages, along
with some real joys, to be found in developing and using your personal power, and you should be aware of them before you proceed.
Many authors and speakers say, or at least imply, that once you're powerful your problems are over; however, being personally powerful in
the ways we've described creates definite strains.

The first strain is simple and straightforward: It's often painful
to be personally powerful in an organization or relationship where

conformity is expected and where there is a belief that everyone should respond to the same incentives ("I'll promote you or love you if you just do this"). While personally powerful people are aware of such incentives and take them into account, they are only slightly motivated by them. And many managers and colleagues find this kind of independence threatening. Ignoring established perks can be almost as disruptive to your colleagues as not getting the work done. In short, when you act powerfully, realize that you may be a threat to the nonpowerful. Therefore, even if you're using your own power effectively, you'll probably need to learn to temper your behavior according to where your colleagues are with their own power.

Second, even when the organization can accommodate personally powerful behavior, the organization itself may be moving in directions that are simply incompatible with the goals of the powerful individual. To use an extreme (though, sadly, not uncommon) example, the organization may cut corners in the services it delivers, threaten its employees, mislead its stockholders, or repress damaging information about its products or its business practices. No matter how good the job seems to be, you may need to invoke your "portability" in such situations and take your power and skills elsewhere, or (in less conflicting situations) remain with the organization and build a life almost entirely off the job.

Third, powerful people can live with a high level of ambiguity, which means both that they don't need all of the organizational supports (and constraints) and that they consequently may be perceived as "free spirits." If you're using your personal power, you may not need an authoritative book ("standard operating procedures") or individual (your boss) or parental relationship that defines what is right for you, that reassures you that you're making the best choices, and that otherwise builds a confining but comfortable box around your thoughts, feelings, and actions. In short, your confidence to live and work without being dependent on these "supports" may make you difficult to work with or manage.

Given that these are just three areas where you can expect trouble, what's the payoff in developing your own power? Here are six clear benefits you can derive from finding the power within you:

1. You will be far better able to control your own destiny. You truly will be more powerful in the one area that counts most: living your life in a way that is most effective and that brings you the greatest fulfillment. (Said differently, you'll stop living for others, while still being able to take their needs, as well as your own, into account.)

2. You will have a clearer sense of what's important and what's not. That is, you will see what is worth expending your power and resources on and where you can make the biggest difference or the most progress.

3. You will develop a keener sense of whether or not you belong in a particular organization. With a good sense of your own power, you'll see where your needs and talents match the organization's, and you won't kid yourself about how they diverge.

4. You will have more energy because you will be applying your power to what works rather than fighting what doesn't work (or worse, fighting to make something or someone else fail).

5. You will do real work instead of spending your time on work-arounds and fancy footwork and office politics. (And the people around you will value you and your accomplishments.)

6. And, most importantly, you'll realize that you carry your power around with you, and you'll stop waiting (in hope or fear) for your boss or your organization to give it or take it away.

With these general characteristics and strains and joys of personal power in mind, we'll now introduce eight profiles that will bring personal power alive in ways that you can see and develop in yourself and in those around you.

THE EIGHT TYPES OF PERSONAL POWER

The characteristics we've just described exist in real people, in you and in others in your workplace and elsewhere. We've clustered the characteristics into eight power types to make them easier for you to identify. A caution, though: These aren't deeply embedded "personality types" (a couple of books in the references section at the back of the book cover that ground, if you're interested). Nor are they mutually exclusive; you may possess characteristics of more than one of the types (although we believe that one or two will be strongest within you). Many of the characteristics overlap between the types; powerful people think, feel, and act in remarkably similar ways. The key to studying the types is to resist the (very natural) temptation to label yourself or others as a particular type, and, instead, use the characteristics as guideposts for developing your own personal power.

So you can begin to do that, we briefly describe each of the eight types and the ways in which their power can be both used and misused. We give each type a title (such as the Artist) to capture its spirit and indicate how this type uses power effectively. We also give a title to the type's alter ego (such as the Loner), who uses the same power in a less effective manner. In subsequent chapters we describe each power type and its alter ego in detail and give some suggestions for enhancing the former (and toning down the latter, if necessary) within you.

The eight types of personal power are:

1. **The power to see the long view.**
   This is the power of strategic thinking, the power of the "big pic-

ture." If you have this type of power, you can see the implications of and potential connections between ideas far into the future (perhaps even beyond your own lifetime). You can give direction to your "commanders" in the field, and you trust them to do the job without your direct guidance. Yet you know the importance of staying in touch, and you communicate well and often with those around you. In short, you're clearly in charge, but everyone knows they have an important part to play.

If you have this type of power, you are a King or Queen. Your alter ego, who has a strategic vision but who attends personally to all of the details primarily because he or she doesn't trust others, is a Controller.

2. **The power to win.**
This is the power that allows you to clearly distinguish and fiercely defend that which is of value to you. If you have this power, you love to "win"—which you define as bringing glory and honor to yourself and those around you and which does not involve making anyone "lose," if you can help it. This power gives you great strength of conviction and loyalty to causes you deem worthy; you think of yourself as fighting for them, rather than fighting against anything. You take rightful pride in your victories, yet you also know how to learn from your failures.

If you have this power, you are a Warrior. Your counterpart, the Gamester, loves victory too, but only when he or she wins and everyone else loses.

3. **The power to support others.**
With this type of power, you are clear about your own values, you can recognize the strength of others' commitments to a cause, and you have elected to use your power to support those who share your convictions. This doesn't mean losing yourself in others' campaigns, nor blindly following them in the hope that you'll find yourself. It does mean that you have made a deliberate choice to

lend your power to others without giving up who you are. (That is, you "have a life" beyond the people you support.) In short, your power comes from your belief that the right thing to do is to work for someone else, and you do that without losing your own identity, strengths, and needs.

If you have this type of power, you are an Aide. Your counterparts, the Co-Dependents, use the power of support submissively (that is, in denial of their own needs). Or they attempt to make others dependent on them so that they can find their own strengths and self-definition there.

4. **The power to change.**

With this type of power, you can recombine what exists into something new. Your power comes from an ability to see the possibilities in any situation, and your main contribution to an organization or relationship is that you can find solutions to seemingly intractable problems, probably by redefining the problems themselves. You can do this because you are able to work with whatever's at hand to improve the situation.

If you have the power to recombine what you have into something new that benefits others (and makes a profit for yourself), you are a Builder. Rebels, in contrast, use this power to make themselves unique, doing things differently just to be different.

5. **The power to create.**

Akin to the power of the Builder (who modifies what exists) is the power to create something new, to perceive what's going on at a variety of levels and to re-present it in a way that others will feel and understand. This is the power that comes from a desire to make something where nothing was before. If you have this type of power, you can naturally see almost everything from a different perspective, one that typically relates more to how people feel than what they think. Thus, you are superb at dealing with the interface (in its broadest connotation) between what's being presented and what others are perceiving.

If you have the power to perceive in unique ways and communicate what you're experiencing to others, then you have the power of the Artist. Those who use this same power to create an island of isolation for themselves so that they don't need to interact with others are Loners.

6. **The power to judge from a moral base.**
With this type of power, you are able to clearly and accurately distinguish effective from ineffective ideas and behaviors. You can do this for two reasons: You have spent considerable time forming your own base of morals and values, and you have come to terms with your inner critic, the voice that provides the "shoulds" about your thoughts and actions. That is, you respectfully listen to that voice, and you request that it do the same for you, but you don't let it run your life. Your goal is not to determine who was right and who was wrong but to bring to the surface more and less effective ways of behaving (in yourself and others) so that they can be examined and enhanced (or diminished) and progress made.

If you have this type of power, and if you have a good relationship with your inner critic, chances are you are a Judge. However, some people with this power believe that the correct moral base (theirs) gives them verbal license to spout opinions and judgments of others at will. Preachers think that their power gives them the right to say anything; Judges are adept at knowing when to say nothing.

7. **The power to heal.**
Can you sense when there's something amiss with colleagues or a friends, even if their physical health seems to be fine? Or can you see in their physical illnesses some emotional or spiritual element that is out of balance? Do you practice the delicate art of acknowledging the fear and helplessness of "illness," realizing that it is per-

haps the most important part of the treatment? If you can see the connection among these elements and how they affect personal health and interpersonal relationships, then you are using a type of power that allows you to diagnose sickness and restore wellness on a variety of organizational and individual levels.

For their ability to go beyond just physical maladies and work with the whole "patient" (including colleagues, friends, and families), we call people with this power the Shamans. Others use this power to keep people sick and to exploit them when they're weak; we call them the Shrinks.

8. **The power to realize deep insight.**
We use "realize" here in two senses: to see and to make real. This is the power that comes with understanding (seeing) that absolutely everything is connected. It's also the power that lets you choose (make real) how you feel about and interpret something. Most importantly, it is the power to let go of personal ambition without becoming burned out. This power may allow you to take on great causes (and to face the powerful enemies that come with the territory) or to simply live with an imperturbable spirit that takes things as they come in the present without conjuring up some pleasant or terrifying fantasy to distract you and drain your energy.

If you have this type of power, you are a Sage. (Although there may be an alter ego to this type, it only operates on the scale of nations, using the power of deep insight to control vast multitudes of people. We don't think you'll encounter it in the workplace.)

OVERVIEW OF CHAPTERS 3 TO 10

In the next eight chapters, we'll take an in-depth look at each of the power types we just described. The key to getting the most out of these chapters is to remember that personal power manifests itself in various ways, and that none of the ways is "better" or "more advanced" than any other (except, perhaps, the power of deep insight—the Sage's power—which may arise after the development of the other types). Also, remember that the alter egos aren't "wrong" or "bad." They have the same power as their positive counterparts; they're simply less effective in wielding it for reasons we'll explain in detail.

To give you a clear picture of the power types and how you can enhance their power within you, each chapter will:

- Start with examples of the power type and its alter ego. The stories that open each chapter are not caricatures; they are real examples from our own experiences with the power types. You'll see that sometimes the differences are subtle, and that the alter ego may look as powerful and successful as the positive type.

  Example: Aides and Co-Dependents both do an excellent job of helping others; in fact, Co-Dependents, more than Aides, often are considered indispensable by those around them. So why is an Aide more powerful?

- Define and describe the positive power type according to the keys to that power (the thinking and feeling behind it) and the characteristics that you'll see in someone who uses that power (the behaviors and actions).

  Example: How do Warriors think about "winning" in a way that makes their combative behavior acceptable?

- Describe how this type uses its power in the workplace and what its relationship to some of the other power types might be.

  Example: How can Artists help in the problem-solving process in any type of workplace? Why are Artists likely to have difficulty working with Rebels?

- Reiterate that the type is human, not a perfect archetype, by giving examples of problems that the type may encounter when using power.

Example: Judges may be too optimistic in their expectation that others have spent time formulating a moral position for their actions.

- Describe why the alter ego looks powerful—but isn't.
  Example: The Controller, like the King or Queen, certainly has a grasp of the long view but loses perspective by wallowing in the details.

- Contrast the fundamental differences between the positive type and the alter ego. (In each chapter we'll give you a quick-reference table of the behavioral differences too.)
  Example: A fundamental difference between the Judge and the Preacher is that the Judge has made peace with his or her "inner critic."

- Give a checklist of actions that you can use to enhance your own power with this type (and tone down its alter ego).
  Example: What are eight actions you can take to bring out the Shaman—the power of healing—within you?

You don't need to go through the next eight chapters in order; there is no progression or hierarchy implied in the way we've arranged the types (except for the Sage, as we noted earlier). You'll eventually want to read about all of the types, though, to get the full picture of the ways in which they interact.

So you can turn to the next chapter and learn about the power of the long view, and find out how the King and Queen use it and the Controller misuses it. Or you can read the box on the next pages for a brief orientation to each power type. You can then select one that you think best describes you, or select a group of characteristics that you'd like to develop within yourself, turn to the appropriate page in the book, and find out how to do that.

The Power Type Finder

If you believe you have these personal power characteristics, or if you want to develop them within yourself	turn to this power type (and its alter ego)	on the page listed
You like to formulate a strategy and lead a group in implementing it. However, you don't usually get into the details yourself, instead trusting your competent subordinates to carry out the tactics. You spend a considerable amount of time communicating with and taking questions from others about your vision and direction; it's important to you that everyone be on the "same sheet of music" about where you're all going.	King/Queen (Controller)	p. 38
The good reputation of your organization and your place in it are very important to you. You pour your passion and energy into winning, but in a way that reflects your professionalism; that is, you aren't focused on beating others or making them lose, but on "triumph" in its larger sense, for everyone involved. You have respect and loyalty for leaders and managers who conduct themselves honorably, but you aren't afraid to challenge them and to take proper credit and recognition from them when they give it.	Warrior (Gamester)	p. 60

Continued

If you believe you have these personal power characteristics, or if you want to develop them within yourself	turn to this power type (and its alter ego)	on the page listed
You like to work in the background in support of a cause or a person you deem worthy of your support. The limelight isn't for you, but you relish the attention and praise your boss or organization receives for a job well done. You focus on meeting others' needs, but you also have a strong sense of your own limits; that is, you haven't given up your own desires in the service of others.	Aide (Co-Dependent)	p. 83
You like to take what is and imagine what could be. Constant improvement and progress are your goals. You're good at taking raw materials and existing processes and making something different and better, to benefit (and profit) yourself and others.	Builder (Rebel)	p. 106
You are known for always having a different perspective. You see things differently, and you see new and unusual possibilities in almost every situation. You can express yourself in a variety of media, and you enjoy the sense of "ah-ha!" that you're able to inspire in others when they are able to think "outside the box" because of something you've done.	Artist (Loner)	p. 126

Continued

If you believe you have these personal power characteristics, or if you want to develop them within yourself	turn to this power type (and its alter ego)	on the page listed
You have a good sense of what's going to work and what's not going to work in most situations. You try to help others (and yourself) understand the impact of actions and words, yet you emphasize what is more or less effective rather than what is right or wrong. You have carefully studied your own values, and you act from a consistent moral (but not moralistic) base.	Judge (Preacher)	p. 148
You can tell when others are in pain or suffering, not just on a physical level but in emotional and spiritual realms as well. You can "read" subtle hints in behavior and words and sense what's bothering someone. Others would say that they feel safe discussing their fears with you and that you are there for them in a supportive and nonjudgmental manner while they work through whatever's wrong.	Shaman (Shrink)	p. 173

Continued

If you believe you have these personal power characteristics, or if you want to develop them within yourself	turn to this power type	on the page listed
You are aware of, and take great joy in, the interconnectedness of all beings and things. You can see causes and effects at deep levels. You spend most of your time in the present and don't fantasize much about "what-ifs" or about how things could be different or better in the future. Yet you aren't daunted by the problems of the present, and you tend to see and promote progress in almost any action.	Sage	p. 192

Releasing the King/Queen Within

As senior managers in an office-products company, Brett and Eileen have jumped at the chance to create and sell a radically new series of products for the (usually temporary) workers who sit at reception centers or "help desks" in large organizations. The product series ("Help Desk Pro") will include such diverse tools as a conference-room scheduler, an automated personnel directory, forms for express mail and faxes, a database for frequently asked questions, and scripts for how to answer the telephone and direct visitors. Brett comes from the product marketing department, Eileen from research and development; however, because of the complex nature of Help Desk Pro, they've assembled a large cross-functional team with experts from every department in the company: legal, shipping, sales, and finance, as well as marketing and research.

Brett and Eileen have established the product strategy and development plans, which they've now turned over to the department heads. The two don't get involved in directing the employees (that's the department heads' jobs), but if there's a slippage or a quality problem, Brett and Eileen are the ones who take the news to upper management. Brett and Eileen are often seen walking through various departments, answering questions, and listening to ideas. In addition, they hold regular communication meetings, knowing that it's crucial not only for everyone to understand the progress and roadblocks as Help Desk Pro develops, but also to see Brett's and Eileen's own commitment to it.

❊   ❊   ❊

Tuesday morning, and Shirley, the operations VP at a bank, is having her weekly staff meeting. The same group of managers she's always had is around the table, although Shirley herself has recently been promoted, as the result of a brilliant plan she developed to revamp the services that the bank offers to customers. At the whiteboard in this meeting is one of the first-level managers in Shirley's organization, explaining to Shirley's management team why his department was 50 percent overspent for the quarter. (His own boss, who reports directly to Shirley, offered to do the presentation, but Shirley insisted that the "guilty" manager be there.)

When Shirley phoned the manager and told him to be at the meeting, she made it clear that he'd better be able to account for every penny, which he has done. As he pauses for breath, Shirley says, "Well, you've only got $20,000 left to go." The manager responds that that amount was spent on an equipment purchase that Shirley authorized. She replies, "You should have spent it only if you had revenues to make up for it. We're supposed to support our customers and make money for this bank, not lose it." The manager quietly, but with dignity, admits that he made a mistake. Shirley says, "Say that louder so everyone can hear."

However, most of the senior managers aren't paying attention or are trying to listen supportively, hoping that this ordeal will soon be over. Shirley's called them all on the carpet more than once regarding the details of how they run their departments. They have nothing but sympathy for this manager who, except for this quarter's glitch, has run his business in an exemplary manner. They know it could very well be one of them up there next week. Besides, this isn't such a big deal—Shirley's department as a whole was underspent for the quarter, so the manager's overexpenditure doesn't affect the bottom line.

✳ ✳ ✳

THE POWER OF THE LONG VIEW

We'll start our exploration of personally powerful people by looking at a type of power that comes from the ability to see the "big picture" and work over time to sharpen its focus, ensuring that it not only survives but thrives. You probably associate this type of power with CEOs of corporations and monarchs of nations (although there are plenty of people in those positions who don't manifest the kind of power we're talking about here). However, that same power also can be found in people who are "just" parents or shop-floor workers.

Our opening scenarios for this chapter do deal with people at higher levels in their organizations, because that's where it's often easiest to see and study this type of power. Brett and Eileen manifest the power of the long view in a positive and effective way. They know that they must bring a new and complex set of products to market. They've developed a plan, which they then entrust to their managers to carry out. They spend time being visible in the organization, communicating and taking questions and suggestions. They are clearly in charge, but everyone's involved. In fact, Brett and Eileen deliberately stay out of the details so that they can scan the whole environment, understand the competitive direction, and keep the ship on course. Because of these characteristics, they exemplify a personal power archetype we call the King/Queen.

Like Brett and Eileen, Shirley has a strategic vision: supporting customers properly and making money for the bank. She wants the bank to survive, and she has a reputation for creating solid operational plans that help it do so.

However, Shirley isn't convinced that the plans will work unless she directs every detail of their implementation. It's not that she doesn't trust her people; it's more that she's afraid that small problems will quickly snowball and she won't be able to stop the avalanche. Therefore, it's important to her to keep a tight reign on everything and everyone.

She wants information (not advice) from her staff, and she expects it to be accurate. She goes directly to wherever the information or the problem lies, bypassing her managers if necessary for the sake of efficiency. She's always on the lookout for mistakes that might sabotage the plan. Shirley has the long view, all right, but she feels it necessary to have a hand in every effort along the way. Because of that, she represents a less effective version of this type of power that we call the Controller.

THE KING/QUEEN AND THE CONTROLLER: WHICH ARE YOU?

You probably see characteristics of both the King/Queen and the Controller in your own behavior. Perhaps you wish you had the magnanimous farsightedness of the King/Queen, when in reality you're up half the night worrying about details. Or perhaps you're wondering why we've implied that Shirley isn't as effective as she could be. (Remember, none of the types we profile in this book is perfect, and some of the behaviors described in the negative profiles seem necessary to get the job done.)

For example, you could rightly say that Shirley's attention to detail and her way of getting information directly from her staff are important for success. They are, but she shouldn't be the one performing those tasks if she's working to keep the "kingdom" together and to formulate strategies for its long-term health.

The Warrior or the Aide (profiled in later chapters) will show you how to effectively apply the type of power that Shirley's using (without her negative habits). The rest of this chapter deals with the type of power that Brett and Eileen use effectively and that Shirley possesses and could use if she weren't mired in details.

As you read about and reflect on the personal power of the long view, you'll see that it's not an either/or proposition between the King/Queen and the Controller. It's a continuum of more-effective and less-effective behaviors. Later on, we'll suggest ways you can enhance the positive aspects of that power and tone down its negative aspects. First, though, let's examine in detail the personal power of the King/Queen.

THE POWER OF THE KING/QUEEN

The power of the King/Queen is within you, in the places where you plan and care for your career, your children's education, your retirement. You already practice "the art of the long view," but perhaps only in those activities that will obviously take decades to come to fruition. The personal power of Kings and Queens comes from their ability to see a larger context ("big picture") and the long-term ramifications in just about everything. Let's take a look at the fundamentals underlying their power to see why this is so.

THE KEYS TO THE KINGDOM

Kings and Queens have four essential characteristics that give them the ability to take the long view:

1. *They are masters of "systems thinking."*
   Peter Senge has defined this for us: "a framework for seeing inter-

relationships rather than things, for seeing patterns of change rather than "snapshots." (*The Fifth Discipline*, p. 68) To a King or Queen, many things are interconnected, and although they may not see the total interconnection as a Sage does, they see enough to know how ideas and people are (or are not) working together.

2. *They see progress on many fronts.*
   Kings and Queens give plenty of latitude to others' ideas and efforts as long as they're making progress toward the strategic vision (keeping the kingdom together and having it flourish). You may see them "allowing" others to make mistakes and pursue possible dead ends; since Kings and Queens can see further out, they may let the experiment go, knowing that it's generally headed in the right direction and just may produce something useful. On the other hand, Kings and Queens often see (and stop or redirect) tiny missteps that, compounded over time, will take the strategy off track.

3. *They believe that everyone can contribute.*
   Kings and Queens are working on a very large puzzle. They know that many small pieces of myriad shapes and sizes contribute to its completion. They also know that it isn't necessary for everyone to be brilliant or expertly skilled or even to have given deep thought to the long-term future of the kingdom. There is rewarding work to be done at all levels.

4. *They have a sustained outlook for themselves.*
   Kings and Queens don't just take care of the "kingdom" at the office. They have taken the same long-term view of their families, their communities, and their own health. To them, these four arenas aren't separate; they're all connected, and the same principles of action apply to all four.

Before we take a look at the details of how Kings and Queens act, we can sum up their personal power this way:

Kings and Queens choose a way of personal power that provides deep and sustained direction for themselves and others.

CHARACTERISTICS OF THE POWER OF A KING/QUEEN

The fundamentals we've just described manifest themselves in ten behavioral characteristics of the King and Queen. As they wield their personal power, you'll see them:

1. *Delegate the tactics to their direct subordinates.*
   The job of Kings and Queens is to set the strategy and make sure everyone's aligned to it ("getting all the wood behind the arrow," as one of our friends puts it). They then get out of the way and let others do their jobs. They check in with and give direction to their "commanders," but they don't try to run the jobs and lives of each individual in their group.

   Example: Sheila manages the Strategic Products Group— about 100 people altogether. She has set the strategic direction for her group: investigate technologies that are three to five years from being stable and make recommendations on how they might be used in future products. Sheila leaves the specific choice of technologies and how they're studied, as well as the definition of what kinds of "products" might result, to her very capable senior managers.

2. *Be out in front, especially in risky situations.*
   Kings and Queens expect innovative thinking from their groups;

if something truly novel or risky comes along, Kings and Queens put themselves on the line first. (This isn't just noble self-sacrifice. With their long, comprehensive view, Kings and Queens often just aren't as frightened, nor do they see as much risk as others do.)

Example: Sheila's been reading about the fascinating possibilities of making products out of super-hardened ceramics. This is truly a technology that's "way out there" and isn't something her group has ever explored. It's just too new and radical, and she knows her group probably subscribes to the very common perception that "ceramic is just pottery, which means it breaks a lot." However, the potential for revolutionary products is enormous. Sheila wants to study the problem further but acknowledges to her group that this territory is completely uncharted. She asks for volunteers to join her in planning the research study. As soon as the plan is ready, Sheila hands it off to a team manager who has expressed interest in conducting this study.

3. *Listen to good advice, regardless of who's giving it.*
   Although Kings and Queens regularly poll their "commanders" for ideas, they'll take advice and suggestions from anyone who has given deep thought to a problem, regardless of the person's level or position.

   Example: One of the new researchers, who until now has done his job quietly and efficiently, sends Sheila an e-mail message describing how he worked on industrial ceramics in college. He thinks Sheila's direction is a bit off and suggests that she explore using ceramics in manufacturing equipment but not in products themselves for the time being. He thinks that ceramic products are just too bizarre for the consumer market, even for five years from now. Sheila thinks that his warning has merit, and she forwards the note and her reply to the man's boss and to the ceramics research team manager.

4. *Talk with their "subjects."*

Kings and Queens are visible in their organizations. They're not there to give orders all the time, and they know that just being available to talk and answer questions is important to keeping the vision alive and the "kingdom" connected. They also know that not being visible can lead to the perception that there is no direction, no leadership, and no concern for the people, their work, or the organization.

Example: Although Shelia's very interested in the ceramics research, she's stepped away from it and has gone back to her regular habit of walking through the group on a daily basis, just to be visible and see what's going on in each department. She's also about to hold her monthly meeting for the entire group.

5. *Take questions nondefensively.*

Kings and Queens love it when others ask questions. Regardless of how naive or hostile the question seems to be, Kings and Queens realize that a question is a sign of interest, under the premise "If they didn't care, they wouldn't ask." Kings and Queens also have an uncanny ability to discern what the "real" question is and get to the heart of the issue.

Example: In Sheila's monthly communication meeting, most of the questions are about the ceramics research project. In fact, everyone remains for half an hour beyond the usual ending time in order to have their questions answered. Sheila is delighted with the amount of interest, even though many of the questions imply concerns about the project. One administrative assistant gives voice to what everyone else is thinking: "Where are you going to get the resources to continue this research?" Sheila responds, "It sounds like you might be concerned that I'll pull people off what they're doing now and put them on the ceramics team. I want to let you know that, if the preliminary report says we should continue the research, I'll go to senior management and get additional resources."

6. *Deploy others to jobs commensurate with their strengths.*
   Kings and Queens can quickly size up people's talents, even talents they didn't know they had. They also provide safe growth opportunities for others to work on weaknesses and develop talents.

   Example: Sheila wonders if the administrative assistant who asked the question at the communications meeting would like to work on the ceramics project but is afraid to ask. Sheila consults with the person's boss, and they offer the assistant a junior researcher position on the ceramics team. She takes it and, to her surprise, likes the work and finds she's capable of doing it.

7. *Give the context for their orders and questions.*
   Kings and Queens, by the nature of their positions, often give direction and ask for information. They know that they'll get the best results and the most useful information if they explain why they're asking and what they're going to do with the answer in the context of the strategy and "big picture."

   Example: Sheila is disappointed with the report from the ceramics team. All the information is there, but the conclusions don't follow from the data, and the team members seemed to lose their nerve and "waffle" on the final recommendation about continuing the project. She wants to know what prevented them from being more decisive; however, she prefaces her request with a reminder about the mission of the department and places the ceramics project in the context of the other technologies that the group is studying.

8. *Form alliances.*
   While Kings and Queens have a "kingdom," they aren't particularly territorial about who can help them. They build alliances that will get all parties what they need.

   Example: The physics department at a local university has a lab that's much better equipped for ceramics research than the one Sheila's group uses. Sheila and the ceramics team manager visit the dean of science and arrange to use the university's lab space for the next three years in return for taking senior physics students as summer interns in Sheila's department.

9. *Assume that everyone's intentions are good.*

Kings and Queens expect loyalty (or why would you be there?). This doesn't mean they naively think that everyone is completely behind the project; however, it does mean that they treat everyone as if they had total commitment. And in the best tradition of the "self-fulfilling prophecy" they often get just that.

Example: Sheila has a disarming way of dealing with cynics. She takes their comments at face value and engages them in a discussion of their ideas. That is, she deliberately chooses to believe their comments are genuine rather than trying to interpret their covert meaning. She usually doesn't get cynical comments more than once or twice from someone who's been through this "treatment." They don't shut up, but they do make more productive contributions to the conversation.

10. *Lead by example.*

Kings and Queens may not necessarily be able to do all of the jobs in their "kingdom." That's a recipe for micromanagement and overattention to detail, which an effective King/Queen avoids. However, they do live by and model the principles that they're asking of the rest of the group.

Example: Sheila doesn't know much about some of the technologies that her group is investigating; however, she does practice the processes and principles of good research that she expects of her team. When she presents information to the group, she makes sure that her data are sound and are displayed appropriately, that the conclusions follow from the data, and that the recommendations take into account the realities of the business as well as the technology's capabilities.

THE KING AND QUEEN IN AN ORGANIZATION

Sheila, Brett, and Eileen, and other Kings and Queens in organizations, provide the direction needed for the long haul. They may have positions in senior management or in strategic planning offices, but you should also look for them in "lower" and less visible places. They may be project managers who masterfully marshal resources from different departments. They may be the employees who seem to have a grasp of the big picture and to whom everyone goes for advice on the strategic parts of their project plans. Kings and Queens will be seen as leaders regardless of the formal position they hold.

THE KING/QUEEN'S RELATIONSHIP WITH OTHER TYPES

If you are a King or Queen, you may have an especially productive relationship with a couple of the other power types. Almost all the positive power types draw strength from the long-term vision of the King and Queen and look to them for direction; however, the Warrior, in particular, is likely to be drawn by the potential for the long-term win that the King/Queen embodies. In addition, the Warrior respects true Kings/Queens and will wish to share in their honor and glory. Finally, a Warrior's attention to detail is just what a King/Queen needs to carry out the tactics associated with the strategy.

Conversely, Kings and Queens themselves benefit greatly from a relationship with a Sage. If Kings and Queens have a long view, then Sages have a cosmic view. The latter see how absolutely everything connects, and they can show Kings and Queens relationships they hadn't considered that might make a difference to the health of the "kingdom."

Two of the less-effective power types will baffle and annoy a King

49

or Queen. As we said earlier, Kings and Queens expect loyalty and assume that everyone subscribes to at least part of the vision for the kingdom—which is not what they can count on from Gamesters and Rebels. Gamesters are great at spinning a story to make themselves look good (a smokescreen you'll see right through, though you'll wonder why they wasted so much energy concocting it). They also switch loyalties based on who has the best deal. Rebels want to be different just to be different. Neither has any sense of the long view.

PROBLEMS OF THE KING/QUEEN

In addition to some potential problems with a few of the other power types, Kings and Queens need to watch out for pitfalls in their own type. Two of the issues are related and have to do with the problem that plagued Shirley: what to do about the details. The third is an issue of "succession." In your desire to enhance the King/Queen power within you, be careful that you:

- *Don't abdicate.* Delegating the implementation of strategy to your "commanders" doesn't mean that you never check in with them. Make sure you have your finger on the pulse of your organization; just don't make yourself the main artery.
- *Delegate appropriately.* Not all your subordinates will have the same level of experience. Some can't just take an order and run with it. For the less experienced, make sure you give direction and guidance more often (but don't do the job for them).
- *Make plans to pass the scepter.* Kings and Queens in organizations often unwittingly sow the seeds of the destruction of the kingdom by failing to have an heir. Succession planning should be part your strategic thinking if you're a King or Queen.

In order to get a complete picture of the power of the long view, let's now take a look at the less-effective twin of the King/Queen, the Controller.

THE CONTROLLER (THE KING/QUEEN'S ALTER EGO)

In the opening scenario of this chapter, you met Shirley, a vice president with an ability to make strategic plans and an inability to detach herself from the details of their implementation. Shirley does have many of the qualities of a Queen; however, her power and energy are siphoned off by her focus on tactics and her less-than-royal treatment of her "subjects." Nevertheless, she seems to have a great deal of personal power. Let's see why.

ARE CONTROLLERS POWERFUL?

Controllers such as Shirley appear powerful for two reasons:

1. *They know exactly what's going on.*
   Controllers know the details of your organization: your budget, the capabilities of your staff, your plans and goals for the year, the mistakes you've made, even what other groups are saying about yours. If knowledge is power, then Controllers are fully charged. However, they don't actually have knowledge; they have information by the gallon, and they're drowning in it. The reason Controllers can't get their heads above water very often is that once they've created the plan, they spend most of their time looking down into their organizations instead of out at the strategic and competitive landscape (as Kings and Queens do).

2. *The only time you see them is when they're charging.*

You don't see Controllers very much. They tend to stay in their offices or spend time only with those few people who they think have something of value to teach them. They communicate by phone and e-mail, but rarely in person. If you do run into them, they may not acknowledge your presence. Often, the only time you see them is when they're on a "mission"—when they need information or when they're investigating (in its negative sense) why something went wrong.

In short, Controllers live in a world of the weak and the strong, the top dogs and the underdogs, and they're determined to be the top dogs who know what's going on. They look powerful because they enjoy using information, which they may do smoothly and effectively. Unfortunately, their downward-looking, tactical approach to power confines them to a never-ending search for the details they must have missed (or things would be better).

THE CONTROLLER IN AN ORGANIZATION

Controllers in organizations cut themselves off from their groups and from the new ideas, new solutions, and new avenues therein. They do this because they're focused on what happened or what's going on now, with little space left for thinking strategically about what might be. In addition, since genuinely new ideas are typically very disruptive of present ways, Controllers have strong motives for rejecting them; something might go wrong.

Nevertheless, one "new" item Controllers often want is more territory. This isn't exactly the power-grab it might seem; Controllers need to know what's going on everywhere, and the best way to do that is to own several pieces of the organization. Once they've expanded their kingdoms, though, you'll find that Controllers retreat again from the group. They live in a world where they can trust and learn from very few people. Controllers especially distrust compliments and overtures of friendship, which might distract them and make them take their eyes (and hands and minds) off the controls.

Now that we've examined the personal power characteristics of the King/Queen and the Controller, let's take a look at the fundamental differences between them.

KINGS/QUEENS AND CONTROLLERS: ESSENTIAL DIFFERENCES

Kings, Queens, and Controllers are all capable of invoking the power of the long view. Kings and Queens have more success than Controllers with this kind of personal power for two fundamental reasons:

1. *Kings and Queens believe they have a right to their position.*
   That sounds pretty arrogant; however, you'll notice that real Kings and Queens know they belong where they are. They're usually relaxed and confident in leadership positions, and their power flows from a sense of self that is solid without being haughty or domineering. In contrast, Controllers are always afraid of losing (control of) their power. Controllers also often have an "impostor complex"; that is, they're afraid someone will discover that they really aren't competent. They keep busy with the details to ward off anxiety.

2. *Kings and Queens know they can't know everything.*
   You might say that Kings and Queens have accepted quantum physics' Heisenberg uncertainty principle: You can't know everything about tiny particles. Kings and Queens chose carefully what they

spend their time thinking about and doing—mostly, preserving the kingdom for many generations to come. They leave the management of tiny particles to others. Controllers, on the other hand, believe that everything will be fine (and that they'll be competent) as soon as they have a handle on how it all works. The unknown can bring doom in the mind of the Controller.

These two differences manifest themselves in the different ways that Kings/Queens and Controllers behave. We've listed ten of these key differences in the box here; after it you'll find some suggestions on how you can develop the power of the King or Queen within you.

Essential Differences Between Kings/Queens and Controllers

Kings/Queens . . .	Controllers . . .
• entrust the tactics to their subordinates	• dive into the details
• go first in risky situations	• go first, with a human shield for protection
• accept wise counsel from any source	• have nothing to learn from subordinates or from less experienced peers
• communicate and spend time with their "subjects"	• stay in their castles (offices)
• see questions as a desire for knowledge	• see questions as a challenge to their authority
• employ others according to their strengths	• pounce on others' mistakes and weaknesses
• issue "decrees" and ask questions in the context of the "big picture"	• issue orders and demand information peremptorily
• form alliances with neighbors	• grab territory
• expect loyalty	• expect treachery
• lead	• drive

Bringing Out the King/Queen in You: A Checklist

Here are our suggestions for enhancing the King/Queen within you and in your organization:

🖊 *Once you've created the plan, let your subordinates do their jobs.*

The King and Queen are relieved that others will take care of the implementation so that they can get back to studying the entire landscape and the horizon.

The Controller worries that others might be doing things that she doesn't know about and hasn't approved. She calls them just to make sure. And she arranges to get the financial reports for their departments before they do, so she won't be surprised in case they don't tell her what's going on.

🖊 *Be visible when risks are being taken.*

The King and Queen make the presentation (or at least introduce it and set the proper context) when their group is about to enter new territory.

The Controller makes the presentation and makes sure all her subordinates are there to take the heat in case there are any questions.

🖊 *Listen to good ideas without filtering them through the person's rank.*

The King and Queen stop in the hallway for anyone who has a well-thought-out idea.

The Controller complains about how hard it is to have a boss and peers from whom you can't learn anything.

🖊 *Talk to your "subjects."*

The King and Queen practice MBBT—management by being there. They tell their groups as much as they can (and when they can't, they say so).

The Controller stays in her office. Her groups say they never see her.

🖊 *Learn to see questions as a sign of interest and caring (and don't take them personally).*

The King and Queen listen carefully and try to determine what the person is really asking or is concerned about. If they can't answer a question, they say so (instead of bluffing) and offer to find the answer.

The Controller feels attacked by questions and wonders why "they just don't get it."

🖊 *See how many ways you can use others' strengths to make the kingdom flourish.*

The King and Queen redesign jobs to take advantage of the talent in the group. (They also encourage group members to redesign their own jobs.)

The Controller watches carefully for others' weaknesses and mistakes that might make her lose control.

🖊 *Always, always back up and give the context for what you're asking.*

The King and Queen say, "Here are my reasons...."

The Controller says, "Just answer my question."

🖊 *Get some partners.*

The King and Queen make alliances with others who can help them and whom they can help in return.

The Controller gets other groups to give her what she needs by adding them to her organization. Reciprocity isn't one of her operating principles.

✔ *Assume that everyone wants to work here.*

The **King and Queen** believe you want to be in this kingdom (or you'd go somewhere else). They use this belief to defuse the cynics in the department by treating them as if they belonged there too.

The **Controller** believes that everyone wants her job (or just wants her out of it).

✔ *Hold the scepter high.*

The **King and Queen** lead their organizations with confidence.

The **Controller** drives her organization with fear.

SUMMING IT UP: THE POWER OF THE KING/QUEEN WITHIN YOU

In this chapter we've explored the personal power that imagines and takes responsibility for the future of the kingdom. We chose to start with this kind of power because it's the one that all of the other power types (except perhaps the Sage) will look to for direction and guidance. Although the Builder and the Artist can also see new possibilities, their vision is more finite—something is built, a work of art is completed. In a sense, Kings and Queens are never done. Their task is to ensure the longevity of a system that, if they've used their power effectively, will outlive them.

As you read about the other types of personal power in the following chapters, remember the strengths of the King and Queen:

- They see where the kingdom needs to go, and they are open to many ways of getting there.

- They stay in touch, communicating what they know, asking for ideas and suggestions, and being seen.
- They trust and honor the personal power of their commanders, subjects, and partners.

PERSONAL POWER STRATEGY #2

RELEASING THE
WARRIOR WITHIN

As a strategy consultant to executives in a consumer-electronics company, Tobey enjoys being "in" with the highest levels of management. His staff, however, is just short of mutiny. Tobey's time and attention always go to the highest bidder—and that's never his staff. (He's been heard to say, "They aren't strategic enough"). He speaks as if his clients' success is due to his ability to help them face and work with "the way things really are" in their organizations. Yet his group knows him to be a master of manipulative and self-serving half-truths. They call him "Mr. Invisible," since he's never around when they need him—especially when something goes wrong because of what he's done. On those rare occasions when he is with his group, Tobey inevitably grabs the spotlight by mimicking (with devastating accuracy) the very executives whose company he covets.

✳   ✳   ✳

It's Monday morning, and a group of engineers have arrived to test their products in the clean room. Nothing's ready: the doors are locked, the network is down, the machines don't have the right settings, and the room wasn't cleaned up over the weekend. Charles, the lab administrator, arrives and takes immediate action to get the engineers working. He opens the room, resets the machines, and recruits his boss to greet the engineers and get them started. While the boss is doing that, he calls the director of network services and the owner of the janitorial company, from whom he requests (and gets) immediate service. When the situation is under control, Charles meets with his team and describes exactly what went wrong. He reiterates how important customer satisfaction is to the organization. Charles has composed a list of action items for everyone on the team (including himself) to ensure that this morning's debacle won't happen again.

✳   ✳   ✳

In these scenarios we see two people who understand the power of winning and losing. Charles lives and dies by customer satisfaction and the good name of the company for which he works. Inwardly, he's mortified by the situation with the engineers, but he turns that energy into action that gets them working right away. He isn't afraid to call on people who are more powerful than he is, and he uses every resource in the organization to win the war of customer satisfaction. He lets others know when things go wrong, then rolls up his sleeves and works with them to find and implement a solution. In short, Charles holds everyone—most of all himself—accountable for the honor and reputation of the organization.

Tobey, on the other hand, wouldn't be there on Monday morning. The engineers are no good to him. They have no information he can use, and they work for a first-line manager who isn't particularly powerful in the organization. When told of the situation, Tobey will say, "That's Charles's responsibility, isn't it?", and in his internal scoreboard will note that Charles has probably lost some points with the boss. Later, Tobey will call the vice president of engineering (whom he "consults to" regularly) and apologize for the inconvenience to his engineers. Tobey will congratulate himself for notifying the vice president about the situation. In short, Tobey will hold everyone else responsible for the loss while crafting a personal "win" for himself from the situation.

CHARLES AND TOBEY: THE POWER OF WINNING

Like most of us, Charles and Tobey both love to win. To Charles, that means working in an organization that has a good reputation with its customers and in which he is well regarded by superiors, subordinates, and colleagues. His energy and commitment to the organization are indefatigable, and he is equally tireless in combating its "enemies" (such as sloppy work). We call him the Warrior.

Tobey also plays to win; however, it's always a personal win, and it usually comes at someone else's expense. Tobey is loyal to anyone who can add to his own power. He puts people into two categories: those who can help him win and those who can't. He hangs out with the former and ignores the latter. Tobey's always looking for the trick that wins, and for that we call him the Gamester.

The Warrior and the Gamester both tap a kind of personal power that comes from a deep understanding of what it takes to win. (In addition, the Warrior can tap the power of understanding what happens in a loss.) The competitor within you probably has both aspects of their kind of power: You fight for the good name of your organization, but you also want to be seen in the best possible light. In this chapter we'll take a look at this power, starting with the way it works positively and effectively in the Warrior.

THE POWER OF THE WARRIOR

The Warrior's power comes from intense loyalty to an organization (or an idea or a person) that the Warrior thinks should "win." We'll first take a look at the keys to this power, including the special definition of "winning" that makes a Warrior successful. Then we'll describe ten specific characteristics of Warriors and take a look at how they wield their power in the workplace.

KEYS TO WARRIOR POWER

Warriors are personally powerful for three reasons:

1. *They have a clear sense of what works and what doesn't, and they'll fearlessly take a stand to advance the one (and defend against the other).*

   Warriors, like Judges, operate from a base of well-grounded values, although the Warrior tends to be driven by a set of definitive rules or ideals, while the Judge is led by a consistent set of moral propositions. This gives Warriors the sureness to adopt "just" causes and the bravery and strength to fight for them, no matter how long it takes to win (even if the victory isn't possible in their lifetime).

2. *They live by a strict code of honor, which they apply as harshly to themselves as to others—if not more so.*

   A Warrior has an unfailing yardstick: Actions either advance the cause or weaken it. One has honor and ensures a good reputation; the other does not. To Warriors, the "enemy" is an idea or act (including one that emanates from the Warriors themselves) that doesn't live up to the standards necessary to support the cause. (But note that this doesn't mean the Warrior kills or fires the enemy— see the definition of "winning" below.)

3. *They have a positive, nondestructive definition of "winning."*
   This definition is so important to the power base of the Warrior, and so distinct from the limited power of the Gamester, that we're going to spend some time examining it in detail.

HOW A WARRIOR DEFINES "WINNING"

You might be thinking about "winning" as the opposite of "losing." Warriors define it another way, and this definition is a fundamental source of their power. The word "winning" is often applied both to situations in which power is used and in which it is abused, but this is what it means to Warriors:

1. *Winning means "worth fighting for."*
   Warriors define themselves primarily by what they're fighting for, not what they're fighting against. Charles is fighting for customer satisfaction. Tobey is fighting against being a nobody in the company.

2. *Winning means "over the long haul."*
   Warriors fight for what will make progress over time, eschewing the quick win. Charles works on a variety of relationships (with his boss, his suppliers, his team) to bring success over time. Tobey tallies his wins (and others' losses) each time.

3. *Winning means "success for everyone."*
   Warriors think they've won when the triumph involves everyone. Charles wants victory for the organization and for himself, and he rallies others to get it; Tobey just wants it for himself, and he sabotages others to get it.

4. *Not winning (i.e., losing) means "a chance to learn."*
Warriors are masters of analysis in a losing situation. Charles quickly sizes up the situation, calculates which actions will have the most impact on customer satisfaction, and takes those actions first. Tobey never loses (by his own account).

Given these four keys, we can sum up a Warrior's power this way:

Warriors choose a way of personal power that preserves what works and changes what doesn't by attacking inadequate ideas, systems, and organizations—but never the people involved with them.

Let's now take a look at specific behaviors Warriors use to wield this power effectively.

TEN CHARACTERISTICS OF THE WARRIOR

Warriors are able to gain victory and honor for themselves and their organizations because they:

1. *Know and use all the rules and regulations in the system.*
Warriors win by knowing exactly what each aspect of the job requires for success. You might say that they know the rules of the game; however, for reasons we've already described, the Warrior doesn't think of it as a win-lose game but as work that brings honor. In short, a Warrior plays "by the book." This means that a Warrior doesn't circumvent the system, doesn't break the rules, and usually doesn't spend time on work-arounds (unless all the routine solutions have failed).

Example: Lori supervises the production of a mail-order catalog for a company that sells books and software. Lori is absolutely committed to customer satisfaction and to the good reputation that her catalogs, and the products in them, enjoy. To ensure that the catalog is of the highest quality and meets her company's production criteria, Lori rigorously applies all the standards from each department that has a hand in producing the catalog. From page formatting to discount pricing to graphic design, Lori knows the people to talk to and what they expect. Lori has figured out how to make all the standards work together to get the customers what they want.

2. *Elicit others' ideas and firmly put forth their own.*
Warriors know that they don't have all the good ideas that will contribute to a victory, so they listen to others' suggestions. However, Warriors won't just go along to keep the peace. They will confidently put forth their own ideas and argue for them, and in the end they will support the ideas that most effectively further the cause.
Example: One of Lori's advertisers wants extra space to market a product that would directly compete with (and may beat) one of the best-sellers in the catalog. Lori wants to say "no" because there is no provision for selling extra space, and it would alter the page layout. She asks her team for suggestions. They are divided on the issue, although most worry that this advertiser will pull out all his ads if he doesn't get his way. After considering the discussion, Lori brings the group back to the central ideal of customer satisfaction. It's important that customers have a choice of quality products. So the ad will go in, but Lori will ask the advertiser of the product that's already in the catalog if she has another product she'd like to market; in other words, both advertisers will be offered extra space.

3. *Stick with the task over the long run, despite interim failures.*
Warriors have a vision of sustained honor that comes from a glorified past and will continue (given the right actions) into the fu-

ture. They don't so much concentrate on the goal (although that's important) as on how it is being reached: Will these efforts enhance the group's reputation or not? It never occurs to a Warrior that "the ends justify the means," unless the means themselves are honorable. And the vision of winning in the long run helps the Warrior learn from (but not dwell on) losses.

Example: The advertiser who already had a product in the catalog is so miffed at having a competitor share her space that she's pulled all her ads and products from Lori's catalog and vows never to do business in it again. As it turns out, that advertiser has some "friends" who have products in Lori's catalog, and they've pulled theirs out, too. The loss of revenue is substantial and will affect Lori's budget for several months. Lori is disappointed, but she's been through this with advertisers before. She reminds herself that she must focus on ensuring that customers don't suffer from a lack of product.

4. *Invite anyone with energy and good ideas to join the cause.*
   Warriors don't think they can win by themselves, and they have no prejudices about who can help. The only requirement is that the recruits share the vision and be committed to working toward it in a manner that brings honor to themselves and the group.

   Example: A college intern who works in the marketing department next to Lori's group has heard about the advertising fiasco. The intern has no experience in catalog sales; however, his task this summer has been to do some research on the needs and buying habits of people who operate businesses out of their homes. The intern is also passionate about the company he works for, and he wants to see its products win in the marketplace. So he approaches Lori with the suggestion that she replace the lost products with products geared to the home business. The intern even offers to write the advertising copy for the first issue. In addition to opening up a whole new market, this idea allows Lori to add value to her existing customers who may also have a home business. Although Lori was initially worried that the intern might just be angling for a good "grade," she now sees that he is genuinely committed to customer satisfaction. She respects his ideas and accepts his offer of help.

5. *Respect superiors who attained their rank honorably.*
Warriors are respectful (without obeisance) to those above them in the hierarchy, as long as the superior reached his or her position in an honorable way. Warriors see such people as having a better understanding of how to win; they embody the good reputation of the organization and imbue others with it wherever they go.

Example: Lori's manager has over twenty years' experience in catalog sales. He started as a door-to-door salesman and worked his way up through the hierarchy by having new ideas that advanced the company's vision. He takes Lori aside and tells her of his experience in marketing to home businesses. Even though her current strategy works well in the home market, it won't work for home-business customers. Those customers expect to see a different kind of advertising and different kinds of specials and discounts. Lori accepts that her manager has more experience in this area and recognizes the validity of his critique. She offers to prepare some samples for him to review. (Her own reputation is on the line with the boss, and she knows it.)

6. *Can sustain their strength and energy over time.*
Warriors work steadily and passionately, seeing in every task the potential for glory in a job well done. They sink their teeth into every new challenge that comes along. And they often come up to speed in a startlingly short time. Because of their focus on winning honorably, Warriors can prioritize extremely well and have an almost innate sense of the order in which tasks need to be done (and how much energy each will take) in order to win.

Example: Lori has prioritized her customers into two segments: existing catalog customers who have home businesses, and home-business customers who don't yet receive the catalog. For her current customers, Lori needs to explain the new home-business catalog section that they'll be seeing and reposition existing products. She estimates that it will take her and the intern a month to create the right look and feel for the catalog. The harder part will be marketing to the new customers. Who are they? What will make them open the catalog? Lori expects it to take at least six months to get this right; they'll need to try out some ideas and see how the customers react (whether or not they buy). Lori executes her plan step-by-step, always keeping in mind that she has a whole new set of customers to satisfy in the long run.

7. *Take (and give) credit where credit is due.*
Warriors like public recognition for a job well done. They have a good sense of what their effort is worth, and they expect the honor to be commensurate with it. They also don't mind sharing the winner's circle and are quick to acknowledge the contributions of others. To a Warrior, the more people rewarded, the more others will be inspired to join such a winning cause.

Example: With the first issue of the new catalog, 25 percent of the existing customers order from the new home-business section. At a company meeting, Lori receives a bonus check reflecting the growth in her business. Lori states that the most important thing to this company is the satisfaction (and repeat business) of its customers. While her own efforts have contributed to that, there are others (whom she names) who helped turn an idea into a winning strategy. Lori ends by saying that the fight isn't over; the company must now apply its energies to reaching new customers. Her obvious passion and commitment set others to thinking about how to tackle this next problem. Several employees who weren't part of the initial home-business group approach Lori after the meeting, asking to join her team.

8. *Learn from losing.*

Warriors take time (but not too much) to analyze errors. They don't hesitate to say where they and others went wrong, but their tone is always one of understanding the consequences, not of blame. Warriors also don't define losing as "being defeated." They look at it as a lack of knowledge or skill, or poor implementation. Because of their ability to learn quickly from failure, Warriors won't be beaten by the same strategy twice.

Example: The first two shipments of the catalog to 70,000 potential new home-business customers have resulted in less than 100 orders. Lori discovers that the order department didn't get the new form (highlighting the home-business discount) into the catalog in time. And the phone operators have been saying "We don't carry home-office products"—because they weren't told that a new type of customer would be calling to place orders. In addition, a competitor somehow found out about Lori's discount and advertised in its catalog that it would beat her discount by 10 percent. Lori calls all the departments together and describes exactly what has gone wrong (remember from number 1 above that she knows how all these processes are supposed to work). She owns up to her part of the error; she discussed the discount with one of her advertisers who also buys space in her competitor's catalog. She describes the impact on the customer and reiterates how this company depends on its good reputation to drive customer loyalty. She presents a plan for fixing the errors and suggests a short-term risk for long-term glory: the next catalog shipment should be delayed two weeks so everyone can be completely ready to support the new customers.

9. *Show up for all battles (not just the ones that they are most likely to win).*

Warriors know you can't attain real honor and glory for yourself if those around you are losing their own battles while you stand by and watch (or are off doing something else). In a Warrior's mind, running from a fight is just about the most dishonorable action imaginable, since it implies at least passive sabotage. In accordance with their commitment to the long haul (number 3 above), Warriors take on the battles so that others can continue to work.

Example: The decision to delay the catalog shipment by two weeks will throw the printing and shipping departments into chaos (say the senior managers of those departments). They suspect that this is a move by Lori to get herself and her group out of a bind, at others' expense. Lori takes a moment to make sure her team has enough direction to keep working according to the new plan. She will then spend some time with the printing and shipping managers. She knows the conversation won't be pleasant, but she will convince them that customer satisfaction is worth some internal inconvenience. Besides, representatives from printing and shipping were at her meeting and are even now working on the necessary fixes to the catalog. Lori admits that she should have involved the managers sooner, but she holds her own in the discussion and doesn't back off her insistence on the catalog delay.

10. *Celebrate victories.*

Warriors work hard and expect others to do the same, but they aren't taskmasters. They pause when the time is right to celebrate and do so in ways that are meaningful to everyone involved. They take a moment to bask in the glory they've created before going on to the next battle.

Example: The delayed edition of the catalog results in several hundred orders. As soon as she has the first month's sales figures, Lori (knowing how much everyone in the group loves pizza) orders a big pizza lunch for everyone who worked on the new catalog. She invites the printing and shipping managers to come down and join the celebration. She thanks everyone for a job well done and reminds them that this is the first step on the road to having even more customers to satisfy.

THE WARRIOR IN THE WORKPLACE

Warriors like Lori and Charles draw power from a sense of duty and loyalty to an idea that they think has merit (i.e., one that should "win"). In the workplace, the strength of a Warrior's convictions will inspire and motivate others at all levels. Their dedication to doing things honorably, and their respect for authority, may help the cynical and burned-out people in your group to see that there is a direction worth following, that there is work worth doing.

Although not as creative as the Artist, the Warrior in your organization often has the courage to take risks where others won't. Warriors may not come up with the breakthrough ideas, but they often will ingeniously implement your and others' innovations. This will be most helpful to you when you need cross-functional or multidepartmental cooperation. With their commitment to glory and honor for all, Warriors are unlikely to let departmental loyalties (theirs or others') get in the way of making sure that everyone is working together for customer satisfaction.

If your Warriors seem to be leaving your organization, take a good look at what you're asking them to fight. Are the tasks lined up with the vision? Are you sending them to fight in continual no-win situations? Warriors will bravely soldier on, but eventually even they get to a place where they'd rather die (or resign their "commission") than see what they value tarnished or cheapened by poor workmanship and a lack of standards. If you feel your Warriors are fighting *you*, take a look at your directives and communications. You may find that you're not fighting them so much as you're fighting yourself—saying and doing things that really aren't in line with your values or those of the organization.

THE WARRIOR'S RELATIONSHIP WITH OTHER TYPES

If you're a Warrior, you'll benefit from finding a mentor who is a King/Queen. This type provides the long-term vision that gives Warriors their context for action. They can help realign a Warrior who is pursuing a tactical fight disconnected from a strategy. The Warrior also may have a close relationship with an Aide, whose more stable, behind-the-scenes approach makes a good foil to the Warrior's bravado and passion. Finally, though they may scoff at the idea, Warriors need a Shaman. This type will show them the value of a spiritual base for stability and inspiration to continue the fight and of emotion and intuition so they can work with other types (such as the Artist and the Sage) who operate from power bases very different from the Warrior's.

On the other hand, if you have a Warrior and a Rebel in your organization, you might be in for some trouble. Warriors see nothing honorable in the Rebel's disregard and contempt for rules and authority. Warriors know that an individual crusader doesn't last long. For their part, Rebels believe codes of honor died centuries ago. They see Warriors as fighting within the system when they should be fighting the system itself.

PROBLEMS OF THE WARRIOR

If you see characteristics of the Warrior in yourself, you have the power, the strength, and the commitment to help many good ideas come to fruition. Be careful, though, of the following three pitfalls in your power:

- Since you have boundless energy and you're always on your guard, it's difficult for you to rest and relax. It's also difficult for others to keep up with you. The cause isn't going to fall apart if you take a day off. If you don't rest, you'll lose perspective and see "enemies" where there aren't any.

- Your adherence to standards brings a predictable consistency to the organization. However, your colleagues may feel that you're forever "testing" them, and that whatever they do, it's not good enough for you. Involve them in setting the standards, and let go a little if their criteria (while not as stringent as yours) still meet the goal.

- Be wary of putting your superiors on a pedestal. You can respect them, but if that respect turns into blind admiration, you may lose faith in both them and the cause when they stumble (i.e., when they're human). You also may have difficulty seeing when they've taken an unhealthy turn.

Now let's take a look at the type who uses the power to win in a less effective way.

THE GAMESTER (THE WARRIOR'S ALTER EGO)

A Warrior and a Gamester both want to win. Both want glory. Both want to be noticed by others. But there the similarities end. Unlike Warriors, who test ideas and systems in order to win with them, Gamesters test people in order to find out who will do them the most good. Gamesters aren't interested in rigor or loyalty; they just want to win in a way that gets the attention of those in power (and keeps others from getting it). A Gamester's perspective is that you either win or you are blocked from winning by someone whose power you didn't take into account (or who has more power than they "should"). In either case, there's always a way to win.

IS A GAMESTER POWERFUL?

Remember Tobey, whose story opened this chapter? He seems to be winning: He's chummy with those at the top, he's always away on important business, and he seems to know what's "really" going on in the company. Tobey, like all Gamesters, creates an illusion of personal power in two ways:

1. *He's fast on his feet (which can be mistaken for surefootedness).*
   Tobey succeeds by quickly figuring out the next angle and betting that it will work. He looks like a confident risk-taker; however, unlike a Warrior, who plans carefully for long-term success, Tobey is just trying to stay in the spotlight. (His quick thinking resulted in his call to the VP of engineering. The VP should thus see Tobey as a good source of information, one he'll call on in the future.)

2. *He's a master of spin control.*
   In his own mind, Tobey never loses. He has an ability to reinterpret events in the most extraordinary (and often believable) way to make himself look like a hero, or at least to make someone else look completely incompetent. Tobey has no problem targeting Charles as the scapegoat for the lab incident, even though Tobey is the one with the most regular contact with the engineering department.

   Yet, despite their apparent success, what looks like power in Tobey and all Gamesters is simply their tremendous use of energy to get themselves noticed. Gamesters only have power in the sense that they intimidate and mislead others into thinking that they are competent and others are incompetent. That is, only the Gamester's definition of winning is valid, and therefore only the Gamester can win.

THE GAMESTER IN AN ORGANIZATION

The Gamesters in your organization may look much more powerful than the Warriors, especially if you believe that powerful people don't fail. Gamesters probably won't be there when things go wrong. In addition, their incredible ability to "find the angle" (and perhaps even lie convincingly) allows them to play the blame game with devastating effectiveness.

But be careful if you decide to hold your Gamester accountable. Because of their ability to cultivate those in power, a Gamester who feels trapped (i.e., has no way to win) may have some allies far up the hierarchy. We've had little success in dealing with veteran Gamesters, except when (in desperation) we've resorted to their tactics by getting the right message to the executives before the Gamester could get there.

A couple of other Gamester-related problems to watch out for: Gamesters will have great difficulty with peers (especially subordinates) who wield personal power effectively. Gamesters can't stand competition, and they aren't above spreading rumor and innuendo to undermine others. Finally, Gamesters won't engage in group-level problem solving. They'll give plenty of "grandfatherly" advice ("I really know better than you"), but they're only interested in solutions that have a personal payback. If they can't be in the spotlight and win, they won't play.

WARRIORS AND GAMESTERS: ESSENTIAL DIFFERENCES

Now that you have an idea of the power of winning, as played out positively in the Warrior and less effectively in the Gamester, let's take a look at two fundamental differences between them, differences in motivation and values:

1. A Gamester (like a Preacher) craves attention and is terrified of being wrong. A Warrior wants glory and is concerned about being dishonored.

    These are very different motivators, though they may look the same on the surface. Warriors have a long-term view of their honor and reputation and that of their organization, and they see how their actions contribute to the cause. A Gamester is motivated to be noticed and must create each situation anew in order to ensure that someone's watching (and applauding).

2. A Warrior (like a Judge) has a deep understanding of his or her own complex set of values. Gamesters have one value: freedom (from rules and standards, from commitments, from authority, from responsibility and accountability, from losing).

    Their values serve as the standard by which Warriors choose an organization to join and by which they evaluate their actions. At heart, Gamesters don't think the rules should apply to them. Even their constant bids for attention contributes to their cherished freedom, since they often get that attention by breaking the rules.

These fundamental differences contribute to overt behavior differences that you'll see in Warriors and Gamesters. The following box lists key behavioral differences that you'll see in these two types.

Essential Differences Between Warriors and Gamesters

Warriors . . .	Gamesters . . .
• use *all* the rules of the system to bring honor to the organization	• manipulate the rules of the system for their own gain
• listen respectively to others' ideas and firmly put forth their own	• feign obeisance to get attention
• are there for the long haul, through good times and bad	• switch loyalties every time a better deal comes along
• enlist anyone who has energy and good ideas for the cause	• ignore anyone (especially subordinates) who can't enhance their power
• respect (and don't fear) superiors who are worthy of their rank	• brag about their relationship with those in power (but make fun of them behind their backs)
• have sustained strength and energy	• have a burst of (nervous) energy for the next win
• take appropriate credit for their role in battles won	• "spin" every situation to maximize attention and praise for themselves
• describe their own and others' errors and learn from them	• blame others for failure, but won't help to fix the situation
• are always present to support others in the battle	• show up only when the chances for personal visibility and success are high
• celebrate winning	• never lose (in their own minds)

BRINGING OUT THE WARRIOR IN YOU: A CHECKLIST

Here are our suggestions for enhancing the Warrior within you and in your organization:

✔ *Learn the rules of the system.*

    The Warrior sits with the phone operators to learn how they deal with customers and to hear what the customers have to say. (How's the company's reputation?)

    The Gamester sits with the operators, and when an executive customer calls the Gamester insists on being allowed to take the call.

✔ *Listen to others' ideas and confidently put forth your own.*

    The Warrior wants to hear how the operators have personalized the "script" that they use with customers. When one of the operators lets the Warrior take a call, she confidently uses her own script. It's slightly different from everyone else's, but it has the same effect: winning over the customer to the company's products.

    The Gamester asks all sorts of questions of the executive callers so that they'll keep talking to him.

✔ *Be present, even when the going gets tough.*

    The Warrior stays on the line when an irate customer calls. She learns how the operators preserve the relationship with the customer (in an honorable manner without giving away the store), and sometimes she offers advice on the solution.

    The Gamester sits with the operators once, but the irate customers get on his nerves. So he turns his attention to the briefing center, hoping to be there when customer executives visit in person.

✔ *Stop trying to do it all yourself, and ask others to join your cause.*

The Warrior finds that the phone-support center is a gold mine of information about customers. Since she can't be there all the time, she asks her team to spend one hour a month listening to calls and collecting data.

The Gamester doesn't see how phone operators can help him win.

✔ *Give your boss some credit.*

The Warrior respectfully listens to the ideas and stories of her boss, who came up through the customer-service ranks. She also tells her boss about any recurring questions or issues that phone customers have.

The Gamester likes to remind (and subtly threaten) his boss by talking about his chats with customer executives (including the personal information they disclose to him, which he finds hilarious). By strong implication, it's the Gamester, not the boss, who has the "real" power.

✔ *Use your energy wisely so there's enough for all you need to get done.*

The Warrior knows what she has to do on a short- and long-term basis and rarely runs out of energy to do what's required for customer satisfaction.

The Gamester goes into overdrive every time a customer executive calls with a complaint. Then he collapses and disappears until the next crisis.

↙ *Allow others to give you credit for a job well done (and return the favor).*

The Warrior says, "Thanks, I think that phone script was a good idea too. John really helped me figure out how to say it all in just two sentences."

The Gamester tells the customer executives how he streamlined the phone support system (by taking calls himself) so they'll get better service.

↙ *Bring errors into the daylight so they can be fixed (without blaming anyone).*

The Warrior notices that the phone operators aren't quoting the new discounts, and says so in the appropriate forum.

The Gamester blames the phone operators for giving misinformation and calls the customer executives back personally to apologize and give them the "real story." He doesn't fix the price sheet for the operators.

↙ *Be there when others need your support (even if they haven't asked for it).*

The Warrior attends the meeting in which the operators propose a different shift schedule. From her own experience, she knows they're on the phones too long without a break, and she says so.

The Gamester shows up when the president of the company tours the phone-support center.

↙ *Stop and celebrate at the moment of victory.*

The Warrior has just heard that the phone operators have won a new shift schedule. She stops what she's doing and takes time to congratulate and chat with each operator.

The Gamester finds a way to take credit for the proposal, even though he opposed it in the meeting.

SUMMING IT UP: THE POWER OF THE WARRIOR WITHIN YOU

A Warrior's personal power comes from a clear understanding of what's worth fighting for (and what isn't). That may seem a bit anachronistic and idealistic in today's world; however, Warriors can help you enhance your own personal power by showing you that:

- "The system" isn't something to complain about and circumvent. It fact, it has quite a few processes and resources that will help you win.
- Being there for all the battles may give you more scars, but it also gives you an arsenal of strategies that ensure more victories in the future.
- Sustained commitment to a cause isn't out of fashion. Changing the world one person at a time adds up to a considerable force after a while.

PERSONAL POWER STRATEGY #3

RELEASING THE AIDE WITHIN

C indy is the administrative assistant in a sales training department. Her manager has decided to bring all of the sales trainers from around the country together in one place (which has never been done before) so they can meet each other and hear the plans for next year. Cindy asks her manager about his "vision" for this meeting: What kind of tone does the manager want to set? What will the participants be doing? Cindy then prepares a detailed meeting plan, including some creative ideas for using the rather cramped space of the training area. (She even consults flight schedules, to make sure no one will miss part of the meeting getting to and from the local airport.)

Cindy presents her plan to her manager. He's astounded. Cindy seems to have anticipated everything, and in the plan her manager can actually "see" the meeting happening. Cindy takes her plan to the other *administrative assistants and some of the trainers (including a couple of managers) and elicits their help in making the meeting a success. As the meeting draws near, Cindy and her team are busy (but not rushed) with last-minute details. No one is working late. When the meeting finally happens, Cindy has time to participate while checking in periodically with her manager and the participants to make sure everyone's needs are being met. At the end of the meeting, Cindy is pleased that she helped her manager and her group looked good in front of such a large gathering.*

❋   ❋   ❋

Mark is the conference coordinator for a nonprofit professional society. He's responsible for planning the society's trade show, which will be attended by several hundred participants and vendors and 20 guest speakers. It's a month before the meeting, and Mark is in a frenzy. He's designing the program, planning the room space, working with the speakers on their sessions, scheduling volunteers into booths and vendors into exhibits, and keeping track of hundreds of other details. (For example, he was worried that someone might think the booth area looked a little shabby, so he brought in his tools and did some extra construction to make it look better.)

In short, Mark knows that if this conference is going to be done right, he'll have to do most of it himself. He was supposed to take time off at Thanksgiving, but he came into the office almost every day to keep things moving. He even spent a whole night boiling down all the conference materials into a five-page summary that would let everyone know what was happening. (He was then a little miffed when he presented the summary at a staff meeting and everyone glanced at it, put it aside, and never asked him about it later.) Mark's coworkers have expressed their concern at his exhaustion. He replies to their offers of help with a shrug and a sigh, saying, "No, no—I don't think there's anything you can do. We'll just muddle through."

CINDY AND MARK: THE POWER OF SUPPORT

Within all of us is the power to give help and support, a special and problematic kind of power that differs from all of the others you'll read about in this book; special because it is the personal power type that is most realized through other people, and problematic because it's difficult to question the motives of someone who's "just trying to help" (however ineffective or manipulative that might actually be).

For example, no one would deny that Mark is supporting his organization. He's doing what needs to be done, and others are letting him do it. (Perhaps they're even secretly relieved and a little guilty; the more Mark does, the less they'll need to be involved.) The problem is that Mark works in a vacuum. He takes actions without determining if they're needed, and then resents it when his efforts aren't appreciated. For their part, Mark's colleagues think they need him to do the work because he's the only one who knows how. The trap here is that Mark won't let anyone else find out how to do the work, regardless of how overburdened he becomes. In short, Mark needs to be needed.

Cindy, too, defines her success in terms of how well she supports others and her organization. Unlike Mark, however, Cindy effectively provides support by finding out (rather than imagining) what needs to be done, and thinking carefully about issues that might arise. Although she's so thorough and organized that she probably could do everything herself, Cindy doesn't hesitate to ask for help. She believes in the importance of what her manager wants to achieve, and her belief is a factor in motivating others to work for the success of the venture. While Cindy doesn't want the spotlight herself, she does need to work for a person or an organization that she feels is worthy of her help.

Both Cindy and Mark embody a personal power that comes from the desire to support others. We'll begin this chapter by looking at the effective use of this power, the power that Cindy uses, in a type we call the Aide. Later, we'll examine where this power becomes ineffective in the persona of the Co-Dependent, someone, like Mark, who tries to make others need him on his own terms.

THE POWER OF THE AIDE

We mentioned earlier that the power to support others is unique among the power types we describe in this book. While effective relationships are important to the success of all other power types, Aides are the only ones who define their power in terms of helping others to succeed. But note: This doesn't mean that Aides define themselves or their worth in terms of others.

The crucial point here is that Aides don't go looking for their goals and values in others; they work those out for themselves, and then they find others who share the same values and whose work they would like to see come to fruition. Aides can recognize the strength and sincerity of others' convictions. And if they share those convictions, Aides are tireless workers who nevertheless find a balance; that is, they don't lose themselves in others, and they don't become cynical.

THE AIDE AND THE WARRIOR: IMPORTANT DIFFERENCES

So far, this power of the Aide may sound quite a bit like that of the Warrior, whom we described in the previous chapter. The two types do indeed have much in common in their support of causes to which they're committed; however, the differences in their power are important, and we've put them into separate types for three reasons:

1. Warriors' power is visible; they're out there fighting the battle in full view. Aides, on the other hand, offer support that's often (though not always) behind the scenes. You'll usually find Aides in the wings, not in the spotlight.

2. Warriors use their power to win glory and honor for themselves and their cause or organization. Aides use their power so that others can win. In short, support is a means to an end for the Warrior, but it's an end in itself for the Aide.

3. Because of these underlying differences in their power, the alter egos of the Warrior and the Aide differ significantly and present different challenges as you develop your own personal power. Remember that the Gamester (the alter ego of the Warrior) wants to win at all costs and literally throws others away when they've been spent for that purpose. On the other hand, Co-Dependents (alter egos of the Aide) cling to others and define themselves by how much they're able to put others in their debt.

However, the most important reason that we made the Aide a separate type is that we wanted you to be able to see and appreciate its power within you and in your organization in its own right, without it being drowned out by the other, more obvious, power types. An Aide's power tends to be overlooked, taken for granted, taken advantage of, and even disbelieved and belittled; therefore, we felt it necessary to acknowledge that there are personally powerful people who consciously choose to support others, not "selflessly" but in full knowledge that their power is most appropriately and rewardingly applied in the service of others.

KEYS TO THE AIDE'S POWER

How do Aides wield their power without getting lost in others' dreams and desires? Here are three keys:

1. *Aides already know what's important to them before they commit to someone else or to an organization.*
   Aides have already done considerable thinking about their values

and goals before they make a specific commitment. In other words, Aides aren't trying to find themselves by supporting others' causes; they are realizing (as in "making real") who they already know they are. Mark hasn't yet figured this out for himself—he's trying to do everything because he lacks a clear sense of what role he wants to play and where his value lies.

2. *In an age when such sentiments are considered old-fashioned, Aides aren't afraid to behave in ways that indicate total (though well-considered) commitment.*

   Aides aren't vocal about it, but you get a sense from their actions and from their perseverance and imperturbability that they've found a home with the person or organization they support. Like Cindy, Aides believe that their superiors are worthy of respect, yet they don't come across as brown-nosers. They also rarely resort to cynicism or bad-mouthing, and they inspire everyone to think positively and realistically and just get the job done—because that's what they themselves do.

3. *Aides truly don't want or need the spotlight.*

   Aides are satisfied and feel success when their efforts help make others look good. They are content to bask in the reflected light of others' accomplishments, and you'll never see them make a play for compliments or attention (although if you're aware of the Aides in your organization, you'll probably find yourself wanting to publicize their extraordinary contributions that just seem like part of the background).

Given these characteristics of the personal power of support, we can sum up the Aide's power this way:

Aides choose a way of personal power that supports others in accomplishing goals that both of them share.

Now let's examine the ways in which Aides wield their personal power.

TEN CHARACTERISTICS OF THE POWER OF THE AIDE

Aides use the power of support to realize their own personal power and contribute to their organizations through ten specific behaviors. When you observe the Aides around you, you will find that they:

1. *Help you figure out what you really want.*

   Aides don't just follow orders. They know the value of true support lies in the ability to help others determine what they need. This enables Aides to supply support in the right places and not waste anyone's time and effort (including their own).

   Example: Emmy takes telephone orders for her company's home-furnishing products. Her manager has asked her to analyze the customers who bought products last year in terms of who they were and what they bought. Emmy believes that this project will be very helpful in showing the significant contribution that her group makes to the company, and she's honored that her manager has confidence in her ability to do the analysis. Emmy is perceived by the rest of the group as someone who just does her job quietly and efficiently, but her manager has come to rely on her as someone who always rises to the occasion, even when it involves situations that Emmy hasn't previously encountered. Hence, he had no hesitation in assigning this project to Emmy. In their first meeting, Emmy confirms that he made the right decision. She helps him define not only what data he wants her to gather (she thought of some statistics that he hadn't considered looking at) but also how he'd like to sequence the report and display the graphics. The manager has a much better sense of what he wants and exactly what Emmy will be doing after talking with her.

2. *Find a way to do it or do it better.*

   Aides define "support" as "making it work." They will work behind the scenes (without bothering you) to find ways around im-
   passes, or to find new and better ways to get you what you need.
   (However, if they truly get stuck they'll let you know. Aides don't
   flounder.)

   Example: One of the statistics that Emmy's manager wants to
   show is the geographical location of the product buyers, but he's
   not sure how to show this information. Emmy knows that the
   easiest method—making a table of the number of customers per
   state—isn't a very exciting way to tell the story. So she finds a map
   and figures out how to enter the number of buyers from each
   state. In the back of Emmy's mind, however, she's thinking she's
   seen a graphics program that automatically creates colored circles
   on a map, with the size of the circles corresponding (in this case)
   to the number of buyers in each location. But she can't remember the name of the program or how to get it. She describes the
   program to her manager and tells him why she thinks it's right
   for this project. Her manager vaguely remembers seeing the program used several months ago, and he's able to find someone who
   helps Emmy obtain it.

3. *Know the situation well enough to anticipate real problems.*

   Aides are adept learners. One of the reasons they provide such
   on-target support is that they do their homework, learning
   enough about the situation to anticipate problems (but not unre-
   alistic ones).

   Example: Emmy's group stores customer information in two
   large computer databases, which don't communicate with each
   other. Emmy knows that the information systems group can't fix
   the problem in time for this project, so she doesn't spend time
   worrying about or trying to resolve that larger issue. Instead, she
   makes a list of exactly which data need to be compiled manually,
   and works with the systems group to figure out how to do it.

Emmy can see that this manual process will add a week to the project.

4. *Know you well enough to anticipate what you'll need.*
   Another part of Aides' "homework" is learning about your wants, needs, and styles so they can support you without always having to ask. Aides are good at knowing what you might worry about, and they'll often come up with a solution that makes it seem as if they've read your mind.

   Example: Emmy knows that her manager will be very concerned about delaying the project by a week. (He works for a vice president who interprets any delay or excuse as a sign of weakness.) The VP wants to see those data that Emmy must generate manually; however, some of the other data that Emmy's working on were not in the VP's request. If Emmy doesn't work on all of the data right now, she can get the manual part done faster. So when Emmy tells her manager about the potential week's delay, she also presents him with this plan: She will use the time remaining to prepare a "draft" report that contains only the data that the VP wants. Her manager can present that to the VP, which will buy Emmy the time she needs to compile the rest of the statistics that her manager wants. The manager is relieved that (once again) she seems to have anticipated exactly what his concerns would be, and has made a viable proposal that will keep him and his group in the VP's good graces.

5. *Check back to make sure you're getting what you need.*
   Aides' power gives them the self-confidence to do quite a bit on their own, but they don't go too long without checking in to see that you're getting the support you need. They keep you informed of what they're doing for you, without flooding you with unnecessary communications.

   Example: Emmy knows that her manager is trying not to bother her while she's working on the project (although he's intensely curious about the data); however, she also knows that he took a risk in giving this project to someone as inexperienced in statistics as she is. So once a day, Emmy drops her manager a note in which she reports her progress and lets him know what she's thinking about doing with the data. The manager always replies to her notes, sometimes with just a "Thanks!" and sometimes with a minor correction to her thinking or a new idea that her note has given him.

6. *Get help when they need it.*

   Aides know their limits. They know that they can't do everything for you themselves, so they delegate tasks and get help when they need it. (And they have no fear of eliciting help from those above them in the hierarchy or elsewhere in the organization, if necessary.)

   Example: Emmy has obtained the graphics program that will display the geographical data on a map; however, she has no time to learn the program, enter the data, and still get the project done on time. So she asks one of her coworkers to enter the data into the program's worksheet, and then asks the manager of the information systems group (who is known as a graphics whiz) to draw the graph for her. Since Emmy made the two tasks small enough so that they wouldn't be too time-consuming, the coworker and the manager are happy to help.

7. *Work to make everyone look good.*

   Although Aides select people and organizations to support based on their own needs and values, once the selection is made, Aides aren't stingy about who gets their help. Aides understand others' success criteria (not just their own) and work to help everyone succeed.

   Example: Emmy needs to have her coworker and the information systems group manager do their tasks correctly on the first try; there just isn't time to have them flounder or do the work over again. She also knows that if the tasks take too long, these two won't be able to help her. So she makes an appointment to see both of them together, briefly explains how their two parts of the project fit together, and stays around to answer their questions so that they don't make false starts. Emmy makes sure that her manager knows how her coworker and the information systems group manager have helped her.

8. *Take care of themselves, too.*
   Aides apply the power of support to their own well-being. They rest without feeling guilty that they've "abandoned" you, and they return quickly with their support power recharged.
   Example: A week before the project due date, Emmy realizes that all of the data and graphs seem to be just a pile of numbers, and that she's getting annoyed at having to look at them. She knows that she needs to step away from the project temporarily in order to regain her perspective; so she takes a day off (instead of just pushing to get the project over with). She explains to her manager what she's feeling, what remains to be done, and how this one day off will help her finish the project in a thoughtful manner.

9. *Enjoy the group's success.*
   Aides are fulfilled when their power has helped others succeed. They'll come to the celebration, but they'll probably sit and talk quietly, watching others enjoy the limelight.
   Example: At a staff meeting after the project is over, Emmy's manager tells the group the VP was so fascinated with the customer analysis that he spent twice as much time as expected going over the report. Thanks to Emmy (says the manager), he and the group have enhanced their standing with the VP. Emmy takes the praise graciously, acknowledges all of those who helped her on the project, and retires to her seat while the others

continue to gather around the manager and discuss the VP's positive reaction to the work.

10. *Inspire trust and confidence in themselves and others.*

Aides get it done without fanfare. They know their support is valuable, and they can inspire others to provide help in a genuine manner without being subservient.

Example: Emmy's success has reinforced what her manager already knew: that she can tackle new projects and figure out how to get them done. The way she did the project has also caused some of her coworkers to pause and look at her (and themselves) in a new light. Emmy believed in what she was doing, she kept her manager informed, and she didn't hog all the glory when it was over. Maybe they'll try a little of Emmy's style on their next project.

THE AIDE IN THE WORKPLACE

The characteristics of Aides that we've just described have some specific implications for your workplace. Remember that Aides have decided the best way to express their values is to support you and your organization. Therefore, their main contribution to your group is their ability to support you without losing their own identity, strengths, and needs. They are good models to have around, since they demonstrate some qualities that are in short supply in many workplaces today: unobsequious commitment, a noncynical attitude, and a lack of desire for personal aggrandizement.

Unfortunately, we believe Aides are an endangered species in the workplace. They tend to be quiet, and they often fill support roles, both of which make them prime targets in downsizings. ("Out of sight, out of mind" and "We don't need administrative help," just to name a couple of common excuses.) However, if you lay off an Aide, you're apt to discover a gaping hole in how work gets done in your organization. One of the great strengths of Aides is that they shield you from the details so that you can do the strategic thinking and cross-functional networking that keeps the organization afloat. We don't suggest that you get to know all of the minutiae of your Aide's job; however, we do suggest you make sure that others know what the Aide is doing for them, and provide regular reward and recognition (privately or in small groups) to acknowledge the Aide's contribution.

THE AIDE'S RELATIONSHIP WITH OTHER TYPES

As you might imagine from what we've said already, Aides and Warriors are likely to have a close and productive relationship. Warriors need someone "back home" to take care of the daily routine, and Aides need Warriors to lead the charge and do the more public and vocal part of the job. Similarly, Kings and Queens will find that the Aide's attention to detail and thorough knowledge of the situation free them to work on the strategy, confident in the knowledge that the tactics will be taken care of by the Aide.

On the other hand, this willingness to work for others puts Aides in danger of being taken advantage of by the well-disguised insincerity of the Gamester (the alter ego of the Warrior). Gamesters are persuasive, and they can get Aides to do a tremendous amount of work for them—though once Gamesters are unmasked, Aides will leave them immediately (often leaving the Gamesters, who now can't get anything done, pleading with the Aides to come back).

The Aide may also have a problem with the Shrink (alter ego to the Shaman). Shrinks just can't believe that anyone would use their power primarily for someone else's benefit, and they'll try to psych out the Aide to find out what the latter really wants (in the hope of being able to use that information for their own personal advancement). Shrinks are also jealous of the Aide's closeness to those in power; they covet the role of trusted confidantes that Aides earn through their belief in and commitment to the boss.

Finally, Controllers (the alter ego of Kings and Queens) may think it would be great to have Aides around to carry out their orders unquestioningly. However, since Controllers really want submission rather than support, Aides will be in for a hard time when their value position conflicts (as it inevitably will) with the closed and intractable position of the Controller.

PROBLEMS OF THE AIDE

Because Aides tend to be the unsung heroes of an organization, their power can cause three problems for them. You need to be aware of these as you develop the Aide within you so that your power of support doesn't become a tool to put others in your debt. (This is a characteristic of the Co-Dependent, whom we'll describe in a moment.) Also, if you manage or work with Aides in your organization, you need to understand where these power types have trouble (since they may not speak up loudly enough on their own behalf). The three problems inherent in Aide power are:

- *Being reluctant to just walk away.*
  As we've already seen, some of the less effective power types (the alter egos) can be quite adept at taking advantage of the Aide's support. The Aide within you or in your organization may need help in seeing that these types just don't deserve the genuine support Aides offer, even if they have chosen the larger cause or organization as a place worthy of their power.

- *Taking on too much.*
  Aides sometimes take (not make) more work for themselves than is necessary in order to provide the support you need, especially if they are the only "Aide" in the organization. (This

doesn't mean they're working overtime, but it may mean that they're working on tasks that others should be doing and aren't.)

- *Being invisible.*

  As we've mentioned before, Aides are in real danger of going unnoticed until they leave—when you'll suddenly discover how much they were doing for you. If you're an Aide, use some mechanism (monthly reports, notes to your boss, or just talking more about your work) to advertise your contributions a little more. If you work with Aides, draw them out about what they're doing, and check with others (since Aides' support tends to be more widespread than you'll ever know from just talking with them).

Now that we've described the full power of Aides, let's look at their alter ego, the Co-Dependent.

THE CO-DEPENDENT (THE AIDE'S ALTER EGO)

As we've seen, Aides are personally powerful in a way that allows them to realize their own values and needs by genuinely supporting and working for the success of others. Unfortunately, this power can also be used by individuals who don't know what they want and don't know where their true value lies. In such people you'll see behavior that involves quite a bit of "busy-ness" without any clear sense of why the person is giving you all this "support." This is the power of the Co-Dependent.

Co-Dependents are addicted to self-sacrifice. Serving other people has become the only way to meet their own (usually unacknowledged) desires. Unlike Aides, Co-Dependents lose themselves in a person or an organization, hoping that the more they do, the more likely they (and others) will find something worthwhile in them.

ARE CO-DEPENDENTS POWERFUL?

Co-Dependents appear to wield incredible power because they can get so much done for you. A "good" Co-Dependent is always doing things for others, making others believe that they need their services. (Hence the label Co-Dependent—you become dependent on what they do, and they depend on being able to provide it to you. It's like helping someone feed or mask an addiction, which is where the term originated.) You'll find it hard to argue with the sincerity and support you seem to get from Co-Dependents. They "just want what's good for you (or the company)," and their power over you comes from their ability to maneuver you into thinking that they're right (and therefore indispensable).

However, this doesn't mean that Co-Dependents are powerful. In fact, Co-Dependents rob power from others (by doing everything for them) and from themselves (by not identifying and working for what they really want). Co-Dependents have enslaved themselves into trying to please, but they really don't know what that means, either in terms of pleasing themselves or others. You'll often hear a Co-Dependent complain, "Nothing I do is enough," when in fact almost anything they do is too much because it's probably done in a random, directionless way. While Aides use their power to focus support where it's needed, Co-Dependents scatter their power, just hoping to hit the mark.

THE CO-DEPENDENT IN THE WORKPLACE

Since Aides know where to apply their support power, they can do so and then "go home"; that is, they clearly have a life outside work. In contrast, Co-Dependents such as Mark work constantly, doing the behind-the-scenes chores that keep the place afloat and that allow others to do the "important work" (as they will self-effacingly remind you at every opportunity). Co-Dependents are always overloaded, yet when you offer to reduce their workload they have two inarguable lines: "Someone has to do it" and "I've already got it taken care of."

On the other hand, you won't often hear a Co-Dependent say "I want." They don't know what they want, or they're so afraid you'll say "no" that they tend to hide their own needs by claiming to speak for "the group." A couple of Co-Dependents we know often use the lines "Some are feeling. . ." or "There's talk that. . . ." This maddening use of the passive voice at first sounds like a legitimate desire to report anonymous information, and can make you (and the group) feel that there's an undercurrent of discontent—until you realize the Co-Dependent is presenting his or her own needs surreptitiously.

Let's now take a look at the Aide and the Co-Dependent together to further differentiate their effective and ineffective uses of the power of support.

AIDES AND CO-DEPENDENTS: ESSENTIAL DIFFERENCES

Why do Aides succeed in providing valuable support while Co-Dependents keep on giving without getting much in return? We believe there are two fundamental reasons:

1. *Aides know what they want; Co-Dependents haven't a clue.*
   If this sounds harsh, try to remember the last time a Co-Dependent you know was actually happy with the outcome of what he or she did. They aren't happy because they haven't made the connection (for themselves or anyone else) between what they're doing and what's wanted. Co-Dependents think, "If I just do this, everything will be OK; they'll like/love me, etc." and then end up won-

dering why whatever they do isn't enough or keeps missing the mark.

2. *Aides are secure; Co-Dependents aren't.*
   Aides know where their talents and skills lie, and they get help when they don't know how to do something. Co-Dependents, on the other hand, often come across as confident know-it-alls. They're worried that if they can't keep you coming to them for the answers, maybe you won't come to them at all. Unlike Aides, Co-Dependents aren't really interested in supporting others, just in keeping others around. Since Co-Dependents look to others for their own sense of self, not having others nearby means losing their own identitfy.

These fundamental differences become visible in the typical behaviors of the Aide and the Co-Dependent, which we've contrasted in the box on the next page.

Essential Differences Between Aides and Co-Dependents

Aides...	Co-Dependents...
• help you define what you want	• know what's best for you
• find ways to improve the situation	• resign themselves to the situation
• accurately anticipate problems	• solve problems you didn't know you had
• delight you by "reading your mind"	• do things for you (whether you want them to or not)
• ask you if they've met your needs	• resent it when you're not pleased with (or don't notice) what they've done for you
• delegate, and ask for help	• do it all themselves
• help to make everyone look good	• punish you if you don't live up to their (private) standards
• take as good care of themselves as they do of you	• neglect their own health "for you"
• say "we did it!"	• sigh "we got through it"
• inspire trust	• inspire guilt

BRINGING OUT THE AIDE IN YOU: A CHECKLIST

Now that you understand the characteristics of the Aide and the Co-Dependent, how can you develop your own Aide power and avoid falling into Co-Dependency? Here are our suggestions for bringing out the Aide within you and in your organization:

Don't be afraid to ask "What do you want?"

The Aide finds out what others (including himself) would be most comfortable doing for a holiday celebration.

The Co-Dependent decides that the group will go out to lunch for their holiday celebration, and is pleased that she has surprised everyone when she mentions that she's already picked the restaurant and made the reservations.

Look for ways to give support through an impasse.

The Aide (continuing the "holiday party" example) figures out how the group can do the two most popular activities—lunch, followed by a movie—for their celebration (since they couldn't agree on one activity).

The Co-Dependent resigns herself to the lunch being less than perfect, since some people have said that they can't be there at the time she's chosen.

Look ahead to see if there are any (real) barriers.

The Aide knows that parking will be a problem and suggests that the group members form their own carpools.

The Co-Dependent hasn't checked on the parking but arranges for carpools anyway, and agonizes for days over who should ride with whom. She revises the lists several times.

🗸 *Give the people you support what you know they'll need, even though they may not have asked for it specifically.*

The Aide provides written directions and maps before the lunch, knowing that some in his group need pictures, some need words, and some feel more comfortable if they know the route ahead of time.

The Co-Dependent prepares small personalized party favors for each person, and she has the seating plan all worked out so that everything will be "just right" when the group arrives for lunch.

🗸 *Check in to see if your support is on target.*

The Aide asks if the plans so far seem reasonable to everyone. He discovers that two members of the group need vegetarian meals. (Even though he'd anticipated everything else, he forgot to ask about special meals.)

The Co-Dependent is hurt when people arrive at lunch and move the name cards and sit in different places than she'd planned. Worse yet, they're ignoring the party favors.

🗸 *Ask for help (it's a sign of strength, not weakness).*

The Aide delegates some tasks to his colleagues so that everyone (including him) can enjoy the celebration without being sidetracked by too many details.

The Co-Dependent made all of the reservations, hand-printed the name cards, and bought holiday table decorations (the restaurant's were insufficient); she's almost late to the lunch because the carpools had to be rejuggled at the last minute. She just did it all herself because (she says) she didn't want anyone else to have to do anything.

🗸 *Help everyone succeed.*

The Aide, as he's going out the door to the lunch, quickly calls the restaurant to confirm the number of guests and to make sure the special meals will be ready. Knowing a couple of his coworkers will be late, he unobtrusively saves seats and menus for them so they can fit right in as soon as they arrive.

The Co-Dependent mentions several times during the meal that, since the name cards were rearranged, "some people are upset because they didn't get to sit where they wanted."

✔ *Support yourself, too.*

The Aide, whose planning has now come to fruition without a hitch, relaxes and enjoys the lunch. By the end of the meal, he's had an opportunity to spend a few moments with everyone, which is very important to him. Talking directly and individually with people makes him feel connected to the group.

The Co-Dependent stayed late last week to finish up the party favors and name tags, even though she wasn't feeling well. She can rest when it's all over (but then there will be something else to do).

✔ *Take pleasure in what you and others have done with your help.*

The Aide leaves the movie (after the lunch) having thanked his coworkers, who helped with the details, and feeling content that he and everyone else had an enjoyable afternoon.

The Co-Dependent goes back to the office and collapses at her desk, saying, "Well, we got through another holiday lunch."

✔ *Notice how others respond to your support.*

The Aide knows that the lunch and movie were not critical to the business success of the group; however, he senses that, once again, the group knows they succeeded (even at fun) with his help.

The Co-Dependent's colleagues are sorry they didn't help with the party plans again this year. They might have had the event they really wanted (and the Co-Dependent wouldn't be so exhausted) if everyone had helped.

SUMMING IT UP: THE POWER OF THE AIDE WITHIN YOU

We urge you to study the power of the Aide carefully. As we mentioned at the beginning of this chapter, the power of support brings with it a couple of unique problems: You need to discover how to wield this power without falling into Co-Dependent behaviors, and you need to watch out for signs of Co-Dependency in the Aides who support you. This is the only kind of personal power with an alter ego that is so closely related—and so capable of appearing positive and helpful.

To bring out the special (and much-needed) power of the Aide in yourself and others, remember these keys:

- Supporting others doesn't mean abdicating your own desires. Be clear to yourself and others about where you stand and what you want.
- You're not going to lose yourself (or become some spineless brown-noser) when you choose to support others. If you're certain about your own values and needs, supporting someone else who has the same goals will reaffirm your identity, not bury it.
- Supporting others doesn't mean doing everything for them. As an Aide, you probably won't get as much done as a Co-Dependent; however, you'll be more effective because you'll only be working on the difference between what others need and what they can do themselves, rather than doing it all.

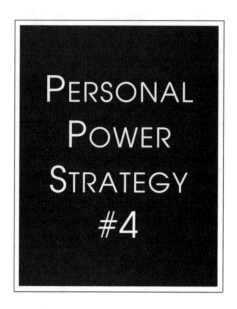

RELEASING THE BUILDER WITHIN

Bruce doesn't like the way things work in the auto shop where he's a mechanic. He keeps trying to do the job differently—ordering parts from new suppliers, working on various parts of the car (not just on what the customer and the owner thought was wrong)—so that the owner can see the superiority of his ideas. Bruce suggests one new idea after the other, hoping that someone will listen. He knows he's been labeled as a troublemaker, but he just can't give in and be the toady he believes the other mechanics have become just to keep their jobs.

✳   ✳   ✳

Cheryl manages a team of engineers who custom-build computers for highly technical businesses. A major bottleneck in the process is the time it takes Cheryl's team to load software onto the computers. After *studying the process for months, Cheryl invents a way to reconfigure existing equipment so that it can "blast" the software onto several computers at once, in one-tenth the time. She turns her invention over to her engineers, who fine-tune it and implement it under her guidance.*

CHERYL AND BRUCE: THE POWER OF CHANGE

In our opening scenarios, you see two people who have a type of personal power based on an ability to change the way things work. Both know there's something wrong with the current situation, and both have ideas for making it better. Yet Cheryl and Bruce get very different results because of the way they use their power to try to bring about the change.

Cheryl's character, whom we call the Builder:

- studies the situation carefully to understand what works and what doesn't
- uses the tools that are at hand
- focuses on making progress by improving the situation
- sticks with her task over the long haul

Bruce, who personifies the type we call the Rebel, wastes his power to change the situation because he:

- focuses only on what's wrong with the current situation
- doesn't do the existing job correctly before making suggestions
- wants work done differently without giving reasons for the change
- is afraid of becoming like everyone else

You may see some of Cheryl and Bruce in yourself. We all have a desire to change our lives and workplaces for the better. We want to leave our mark by changing the landscape, if only in some small way. While many of us don't have the wildly creative skill of the Artist, we do have a longing to make a difference. And sometimes we also want to break the rules, not just to make a difference but to be different. That urge to stand out in the crowd can give us a feeling of tremendous strength or tremendous loneliness, depending on how we use the power behind the urge.

In this chapter, we'll take a look at the type of personal power that stems from an ability to effect change. We'll start with the Builder, who effectively uses power to make progress by positively altering the environment.

THE PERSONAL POWER
OF THE BUILDER

Builders are always looking for ways to make things better. They see possibilities where others see only roadblocks. To get past the roadblocks, Builders use their uncanny ability to reconfigure, recombine, and repurpose *what's already in the environment* to come up with a solution. They make no assumptions about the limitations of people or objects. Builders are the ones who will use the mundane, even scrap, materials on hand and make something useful from them.

Lest you think that having the power of a Builder isn't very exciting, let's take an example in which "Builder thinking" saved lives, probably where none of the other power types could have. As the Apollo 13 disaster unfolded, it became apparent that the crew would die from their own exhaled carbon dioxide if an air filter couldn't be improvised. Spacecraft engineers had all sorts of ideas for making the filter—until the flight controller reminded them, "Don't use anything that they don't have." In short, he asked the engineers to go into Builder mode, to focus on what the crew already had and to work around the clock to come up with something new that would save three men's lives. To sum it up:

Builders choose the path of personal power that enables them to take ideas (their own and others') and turn them into reality.

THE PRINCIPLE BEHIND BUILDER POWER

The driving force behind the power of the Builder is the ability to take what exists and make something new. John Seely Brown calls this "radical incrementalism," and he defines it as making dramatic progress by using what's already available. The Builder's power stems from being able to create something new by incrementally changing what is; however, "incremental" doesn't necessarily mean ordinary or predictable. Repurposing a drinking tube to be a hose in an air filter, as in the Apollo 13 example we cited earlier, doesn't change the tube's original purpose as a holder of nonsolid substances. What is radically different is the effect of the tube in its new job: passing air to and from the filter so that people can breathe, rather than just passing juice to their mouths.

If you're a computer user, you're already familiar with (and you probably greatly appreciate) another example of this Builder-like ability to use what exists in new and better ways. "Backwards compatible" is a term used by programmers to indicate that their software will work with documents created in earlier versions of the program, or will work with previous versions of the operating system, or will run on older hardware. Although many programmers probably are Artists (or Rebels) at heart, they know that for the sake of your costly investment, they must be Builders and ensure that what's new works with what isn't. In short, Builders operate from the axiom "Work smarter, not harder."

KEYS TO BUILDER POWER

How do Builders succeed with just what's available? By saying to themselves (and others):

1. *I can improve it.*
   Builders believe they can make life better for themselves and others, but they aren't cockeyed optimists, and they aren't arrogant. The key to their power is that, with almost childlike naiveté, they believe that anything can be improved, that people and objects have capabilities beyond what they're defined (or stereotyped) as.

2. *I can do it.*
   Builders are confident. Without arrogance and self-aggrandizement, they believe in their capacity to make the situation better. Since Builders rarely close down options permanently, they have a track record of success where others said it couldn't be done.

3. *I will profit by it.*
   Builders want to make progress for themselves, as well as improve others' lot. They take pride in accomplishments that are achieved *with* and *for* others, but they're careful not to do anything *to* others just "for their own good." Builders want everyone to experience an improved environment, and they (quite naturally) want the credit and benefits that accrue to having created the new ideas that move society and organizations along.

WHAT DOES BUILDER POWER LOOK LIKE?

In our opening scenario, Cheryl improved a process and cleared a roadblock by using what she had (equipment and personnel) in a new way. Let's take a look at the specific behaviors that define the personal power of Builders such as Cheryl.

TEN CHARACTERISTICS OF THE BUILDER

Builders draw on a form of personal power that comes from a desire and ability to make change for the better. Specifically, Builders:

1. *Focus on what can be improved.*
   Builders don't whine about "the system" or some amorphous entity that's at fault. Their power lies in their ability to spot what can be made better, and they succeed because they have greater vision than the rest of us regarding ways to improve situations.

   Example: Lucy manages a training department based in the United States. Foreign subsidiaries of the company want to use the training Lucy's group produces. Lucy knows her group can't possibly translate all of the training, but she does think her group can get the training to the subsidiaries faster so they'll have time to do their own localization.

2. *Invent ways to do things differently to make progress.*
   Builders want to be known for being creative in ways that move everyone forward. They aren't interested in being different just to be different. They know that's just wasted effort.

   Example: Lucy suspects that part of the problem in getting training to the subsidiaries in a timely manner is due to people being stuck in a "time zone" mentality, i.e., work can't get done when I'm asleep. She comes up with a process for sending materials from the United States at the end of the day so they'll be there when the subsidiaries' staffs arrive at work. Then that group will send the work back at the end of their day, which is the beginning of the day for the U.S. workers. In effect, Lucy has just bought herself a round-the-clock workforce with no extra resources.

3. *Look for ways to improve on existing ideas.*

   Builders take the raw materials at hand and make something new from them. The great strength of Builders is that they make no assumptions about what something can be, what it can be used for, or who "owns" it.

   Example: Lucy knows there's already a high-speed network between the U.S. offices and some of the subsidiaries. At the moment, the network belongs to the engineering department and is used exclusively by that department for sending product specs to manufacturing sites. Lucy's department doesn't have access to that network, and neither do some of the subsidiaries, but Lucy thinks she can get permission to add her group to the network so they can send training materials through the existing pipeline.

4. *Use others' ideas in order to make progress.*

   Builders don't worry too much about ownership; they just want to see improvement. Builders will take good ideas wherever they find them, and will accept others' constraints if that means progress can be made.

   Example: Lucy takes her idea to the manager of the engineering network. The good news is that he already has plans to extend the network to the other subsidiaries with whom Lucy needs to communicate, and he can give her space to send her material. The bad news is that, for now, all of the documents will have to be in a particular format so that the network can handle them, and Lucy can only send her material after 7 p.m., when engineering's work is completed. Lucy agrees to use the format and work with the timetable.

5. *Sustain a high level of energy over time to create what's needed.*

   Builders expect to run into the argument that "we've never done it that way before." They also expect that the people and things they're trying to reconfigure won't work as planned—after all, they're using things in ways they weren't intended to be used. Builders keep up their energy through the setbacks and roadblocks by "chunking" the tasks into manageable pieces and by keeping their options open.

Example: Having garnered the support of engineering, Lucy makes a list of what it's going to take to change the training materials format and (most importantly) to change the mindset of some 9-to-5 people she has in her department and in the subsidiaries. In the end, it takes about six months of her constant attention to this project to get it up and running.

6. *Succeed by involving others.*

Successful Builders know they are good at inventing the ideas, but they need others to implement them. In short, they hold on to the goal, but let go of the specific means for getting to it.

Example: Lucy's laid the groundwork for a 24-hour workday between her department and the subsidiaries. She's obtained the tools (the network and the document format). Now she hands the implementation details off to her staff and to the subsidiaries. She genuinely doesn't care (and says so publicly) about exactly how the training materials get prepared in the format and shipped to their destination, nor about who's involved in the process, just as long as the ideas are implemented and the goals met.

7. *Act confidently.*

Builders believe they can make positive change, and their confidence inspires others to believe the same of themselves. Builders aren't arrogant, but they are very sure of themselves because they know they've chosen a problem and invented a solution that's important for more than just their own well-being.

Example: At this point you may be thinking that all Lucy's done is force her own ideas onto her staff and the workers in the foreign offices; however, she picked a problem (sharing of training materials) that was a chronic sore spot for everyone involved, and she used tools that were already in the environment. Lucy knows her plan can succeed because it solves a problem that's important to everyone.

8. *Acknowledge credit appropriately.*
Builders are good, and they know it. They take credit for their ideas without any display of false modesty. They also unhesitatingly give credit to others who bought their vision and implemented it.

Example: At a worldwide training meeting, Lucy gets an award from her boss and from the subsidiaries for her idea. In accepting the award, Lucy acknowledges that she had the initial idea and that she laid the groundwork by working with engineering to re-purpose existing resources. Lucy then goes on to name each individual who worked on the implementation, and specifically mentions their unique contributions to the effort.

9. *Profit by meeting others' needs.*
Builders want to enhance their own personal situation. They want to make money or win awards or gain attention for their efforts. Real Builders know that the only sustainable way to do this is to focus on improving other people's lives as well as their own.

Example: It's important to Lucy that she be promoted to a more responsible—and global—position within the company. To do that, she had to make an impact at a global level. The training materials process she built gave Lucy international recognition *and* solved a major problem for the entire enterprise.

10. *Fight for what they want to change.*
Builders don't give up. They are able to maintain their positive, hopeful outlook because when they fight for resources or mind-share, they are fighting for what they want, not against something they don't want. It may seem like a subtle point, but this perspective makes a world of difference in Builders' ability to sustain their energy over time. They think in terms of moving toward a goal instead of trying to prevent or pull away from a roadblock.

Example: Lucy didn't see an enemy in the status quo (training materials in English in foreign countries) or in the engineering manager who insisted on a particular format and time frame.

She didn't spend time fighting to change the engineer; she spent her efforts fighting for the resources (access to the network and the format) and the mindset (they can work while we're asleep) that would lead to successful implementation of her idea.

THE BUILDER IN THE WORKPLACE

A Builder's empowerment comes from an ability to see the possibilities in any situation. Builders' major contribution to an organization is finding solutions to seemingly intractable problems. They are good problem-solvers; moreover, they often find the solutions by redefining the problem itself—looking at it in terms of what's possible instead of what's missing. (This is the "fight for" versus "fight against" principle we mentioned earlier.) Remember that Lucy defined her problem as the timely transfer of training materials, not as a lack of expertise on the part of the subsidiary staffs.

PROBLEMS OF THE BUILDER

Like the other positive power types we've described in this book, Builders are effective but not perfect. If you find that you fit the profile of the Builder, here are some pitfalls of the type that you should watch out for in yourself.

As a Builder in your workplace, you will be frustrated by an overly controlling boss or organization that rigidly prescribes how tasks must be done and how tools must be used. This will be especially true if your organization hides behind the "we've always done it this way" excuse for maintaining its rigidity (and for hiding from change).

An example that we've experienced involves the powerful and well-entrenched myth that new employees must be enculturated into a new organization by attending a day (or two or three) of classroom "orientation." The Builder in you will say that such orientations are good for meeting coworkers face to face, but not effective in terms of providing tools that you're going to need back on the job. Further, in dispersed organizations, bringing everyone to a central orientation is becoming less and less cost-effective. But just try (as we have) to implement a program that delivers the same orientation information, plus useful tools and at least some personal contact, through another medium (such as CD-ROM or video conferencing), and watch the resistance mount.

The good news is that as a Builder you have almost boundless positive energy to creatively work around these kinds of roadblocks.

You may encounter two other problems in your work and life as a Builder. Both involve the same underlying principle: letting go. First, because of their positive outlook and their belief that almost any situation can be improved, Builders sometimes labor on when the cause is lost. This is a case of not letting go soon enough when there just aren't enough resources or supports in the environment for what the Builder wants to do.

The second problem is exactly the opposite. Builders are quite interested and committed in the problem-analysis stage and in the creation of the new idea; however, the Builders we know have a difficult time sticking with the day-to-day implementation and operation of what they've invented. In short, because of their energetic search for the new and improved, Builders get bored easily when things are humming along.

If you think you have the personal power of the Builder, make sure you align yourself with a tactical operations person (such as a Warrior or an Aide) who can sustain your ideas in the long run.

THE BUILDER'S RELATIONSHIP WITH OTHER TYPES

As we just mentioned, Builders can benefit from a relationship with Warriors or Aides. These latter two types don't have the Builder's ability to see the new and exciting in the mundane, but they do have an excellent set of tactics for implementing new ideas and making sure they stick over the long haul. Another fruitful pairing is the Builder and the Sage. Often, Builders see their inventions in isolation from each other; each new idea is more or less independent from the rest. Sages can help Builders see the larger tapestry in which they're working, and see how the individual threads of the Builder's ideas have common themes and connections.

Builders are going to have the most trouble with Controllers (the alter ego of the King/Queen power type). Controllers suck power from others (especially Builders) by regulating everything in the environment—including others' thoughts and ideas. The Controller's "my way or the highway" attitude will probably send the Builder packing, since there won't be room to change and work with the few raw materials that may have escaped the Controller's grasp.

We've taken a look at the power of the Builder, who wants to make positive change for everyone. Now let's take a look at how this power can be wasted by someone who just wants to be different, in a type we call the Rebel.

THE REBEL (THE BUILDER'S ALTER EGO)

Remember Bruce? You read about his disgruntlement at work in the auto shop; he probably doesn't like the way things happen in other aspects of his life either. He wants change, but if you ask for specifics you'll probably only hear that he doesn't want things the way they are now. He doesn't have a very clear idea of how he'd like them to be. In contrast to Builders, who create a new shared reality, Rebels create a separate reality defined primarily by how they aren't like others.

THE REBEL'S POWER

Is a Rebel powerful? As with all of the alter egos we've described in this book, a Rebel does have power, and it comes from the ability to do something others can't—in this case, stand out. This is akin to the Loner's power to stay out, and reflects both Rebels' and Loners' need to define themselves as separate from everyone else. In both of these alter-ego types, this need hides a deep-seated fear of being swallowed up in the crowd. Rebels, though, are afraid of being just like everyone else, while Loners are afraid of having all their energy drained away by the masses.

Unlike a Builder, a Rebel looks powerful—but isn't—for three main reasons:

1. Rebels are clearly nonconformists; they don't get sucked into the fad of the moment. However, unlike Builders, whose power is spent on standing out in positive ways, through growth and development, a Rebel's power is spent on simply being different.

2. Although they say that they'll be happy (i.e., not angry) if things change, Rebels actually waste much of their power holding onto their anger (since that's what has defined them for so long). You'll see this in Rebels who, having "won" one cause, become listless or directionless (i.e., powerless) or, more likely, immediately seek another battleground. Builders, on the other hand, celebrate change and use the "downtime" between efforts to recharge their power and energy.

3. Rebels expend a great deal of their power in paying attention to others and then affecting behaviors to ensure that they stand out from the crowd. Although their power seems to come from their separateness, Rebels spend considerable energy on "being seen." Their greatest fear is that they'll be ignored. In contrast, a Builder's power comes from the ability to make change for and with others.

THE REBEL IN THE WORKPLACE

If you have a Rebel (or think you are one) in your workplace, here's what you're likely to encounter. Unlike the Builder, who naturally sees and uses things differently, a Rebel's difference is studied and forced *because what he really wants is your attention.* In other words, Rebels love to pick a fight. Their contrariness on absolutely every issue will quickly try your patience. Yet ironically, by defining themselves as different from others, Rebels put themselves completely at the mercy of others. They must carefully study what others are so they'll know what not to be. This can work in your favor if you have a Rebel in your midst.

We once knew an employee who got his way almost every time with his (Rebel) boss by recommending a course of action diametrically opposed to the one he (the employee) actually wanted. His boss—a classic Rebel in this situation—was determined to reject the employee's ideas no matter what, so the employee just took the opposite tack and got what he wanted. We've also had success in dealing with Rebels by calling them on their behavior, saying something like, "Do you really think there's a problem, or are you raising the issue just to raise it?"

In the end, you'll find Rebels' singular focus on being unique and independent to be irrational and confining. They force themselves to stay in a nonconformist space—an oxymoron if there ever was one.

Now that we've explored the Builder and Rebel, let's look at them side by side and examine their ability to apply their power to make a difference.

BUILDERS AND REBELS: ESSENTIAL DIFFERENCES

The power of the Builder or the Rebel is the power to make change. The two types do this in a constructive or destructive manner, respectively, because of three underlying differences that influence their be-havior:

1. Builders can look inward to understand the source of their emo-tions. For example, when Builders become angry (perhaps at the slow pace of progress) they look to themselves first to see what they might be doing to hold things up, or how they might take a more active role in moving others along. Rebels, on the other hand, have a diffuse and persistent sense of anger and restlessness that they project onto other people and situations. They're afraid to look within, to the source of their strong emotions—which have built up over years of repressing or externalizing their hurt and anger.

2. Builders' motivation is to profit by improving the lot of everyone. They have a strong need to make personal gains, but they under-stand that the only way to do that in a sustainable manner is to focus on meeting the needs of others. In contrast, Rebels' prime motivation is to get attention; however, they don't want too much sustained attention in any one situation (hence their constant switching from one "cause" to another), since that might mean that they'd start to care, become attached, become "normal"—and fade into the background.

3. Builders operate from the positive and have a clear vision of where they want to go. Rebels live in a world of the negative, and only know that the current situation is intolerable. Builders are strug-gling *with* the way things are in order to make them better in clearly defined ways. Rebels are struggling *against* what exists, but they have only defined their desires in terms of what should not exist.

These fundamental differences impel the Builder and the Rebel to act in different ways to change the world (or some small piece of it). The box on the next page lists key behavioral differences that you'll see in these two types.

Essential Differences Between Builders and Rebels

Builders . . .	Rebels . . .
• focus on what can be better	• focus on what's wrong
• do things differently in order to make progress	• do things differently just to be different
• improve on existing ideas	• reject all aspects of the status quo (including what works)
• use (and even conform to) others' good ideas in order to make progress	• reject others' ideas in order to remain nonconformist
• have sustained energy over time	• work in fits and starts
• succeed by employing others	• "succeed" by ignoring others
• project confidence	• ooze anger
• take (and give) credit without false modesty	• take credit defensively (but don't give it)
• profit by inventing new ways to meet others' needs	• get attention by breaking the rules
• fight for	• fight against

Bringing Out the Builder in You: A Checklist

So far, we've described the power of the Builder and the powerlessness of the Rebel and compared the characteristics of both types. As you develop the Builder (and mitigate the Rebel) within you, keep in mind the following behaviors that will maximize (or minimize) your power to bring about change:

✔ *Find something, anything in the situation that can be changed for the better.*

The Builder has a tiring commute and looks into alternative transportation.

The Rebel complains about too many drivers on the road.

✔ *Try different options to maximize your chances of success.*

The Builder tries taking the bus and the train, and carpools with a friend.

The Rebel drives to work, still complaining about the other drivers along the way.

✔ *Take what's available and improve it.*

The Builder takes advantage of a remote dial-up service and works from home one day a week.

The Rebel refuses even to try telecommuting—because some others are doing it.

✔ *Ask others for their ideas, and accede to their restrictions if it means you'll make progress.*

The Builder finds out what the local transportation utility recommends and adjusts her work schedule to fit the train schedule.

The Rebel rejects coworkers' offers to join their carpools.

✔ *Monitor your energy level so that you'll make it to the end of the project.*

The Builder gets everything done on Thursday night so she has enough time and energy to drive herself (and sit in traffic) on Fridays, when she must have her car.

The Rebel spends countless hours researching alternative fuel sources and transportation options—and still drives to work every day, complaining about the traffic.

✔ *Put a team together to help you get your ideas implemented.*

The Builder asks coworkers to help her get a "work at home one day a week" option accepted by management for all employees.

The Rebel puts together a "Commuters' Manifesto" and distributes it through company mail.

✔ *Act confidently. If there's something bothering you, get it out on the table.*

The Builder is confident that her work-at-home day is just as productive as her office days, and she confronts a colleague who accuses her of "just goofing off" when she's working at home.

The Rebel resents all the other single-driver cars. Even though he can't possibly do it, they should be carpooling.

✔ *Say "thank you" when someone praises your efforts, and mention those who helped you implement your idea.*

The Builder says, "Thanks, I think it was a good idea too," when others praise her work-at-home initiative. And she thanks human resources for helping her implement her idea.

The Rebel says, "Thanks, but it's not for everyone" when someone admires his electric car.

✔ *Enjoy the attention you got by helping others and yourself.*

The Builder takes pleasure in the bonus she got for suggesting the work-at-home day.

The Rebel enjoys the attention he got for wearing his Rollerblades into the work area.

✔ *Fight for the resources you need to see your idea become a reality.*

The Builder runs for local office and fights for increased alternative transportation.

The Rebel fights against traffic by tailgating other drivers.

SUMMING IT UP: THE POWER OF THE BUILDER WITHIN YOU

We opened this chapter with the stories of Cheryl and Bruce, a Builder and a Rebel respectively. Both had a desire to change their circumstances, and both had ideas about how to do it. Let's recap the power of the Builder by giving Bruce a Builder's power and seeing the difference it makes in his situation:

Bruce, a mechanic in an auto shop, has noticed that customers bring their cars back several times to fix the same problems. Bruce keeps some records, does some research, and concludes that the car problems aren't being fixed the first time for two reasons: The replacement parts are of poor quality, and the problem with the cars is deeper than the original diagnosis typically reveals. Bruce brings his data to the shop owner and suggests that the shop use an evaluation form for parts suppliers, like the one that's used in the front office to rate insurance carriers. Bruce also suggests that the owner spend a little more time in his initial diagnosis of a car's problem. The owner says he can't do that, so Bruce offers to do the diagnoses with him. Two can do it faster and better than one.

The differences in Bruce between this scenario and the one that opened this chapter illustrate the three trademarks of a personal power based on the ability to bring about change. We've called people with this power Builders because they:

- Think positively, and concentrate on what can be changed
- Take what's available in the environment and put it to new use
- Stand out from the crowd by working with the crowd to improve everyone's lot

PERSONAL POWER STRATEGY #5

RELEASING THE
ARTIST WITHIN

John, a supervisor of eight writers in a documentation group, has worked in his office for weeks creating a project-tracking system for his team. The tool is truly unique: although it tracks the usual project-management items (costs, timelines, personnel, milestones, etc.), its most valuable aspect is that it offers new ways of displaying and relating the data so they can be viewed across projects or over time. In fact, John's creation isn't so much a project-management tool as a project-visioning tool. The system is now ready, and John has held a training session in which he's explained the system and how he expects his team to use it. "Just enter all your project information in here," he says, "and we won't have to track each other down to find it."

In the ensuing days, John checks the system daily and discovers that no one is entering their project data. So he tells his team members *that they are required to bring the updated information to their weekly meetings. At the first meeting, his writers grumble about spending more time entering the myriad facts about projects than they spent working on the projects. They suggest a few changes to the system, and John reluctantly agrees, but adds, "Your thinking is driving me crazy." He spends the next two weeks in his office making the changes, adding some enhancements, and even sketching out some other tools for his group to use.*

Meanwhile, all of John's team members complain to his manager about how John "dumped" this system onto them without consulting them and without considering their already overloaded work schedules. "He stays in his office and fills up plates," they say. When John's manager tries to discuss the situation with him, he angrily reminds her of all the business he's brought into the department. If the work isn't getting done with the tools he provides, it's because his team is "too junior." He says he's exhausted from working with people who need so much hand-holding, and he wants some time off to get his strength back and look for other opportunities.

✹   ✹   ✹

Kevin works on John's documentation team. He writes training manuals for complex machinery and occasionally teaches classes on the theoretical and technical underpinnings of the machines. Kevin has a reputation as a gifted writer and teacher who constantly puts his work-in-progress out for others' comment, and who creates final products that inspire his students and readers to care about the topic, not just understand it.

One of the keys to Kevin's success is that he can create analogies that relate complicated concepts to objects and processes that his students already know and understand. (One time, when his class was struggling to understand how a modem converts digital and analog signals, Kevin had the students think of their chairs as ferry boats and had them "sail" from one side of the room to another, taking on "digital" passengers and letting off "analog" passengers at each end of the voyage across "Analog Bay.") Kevin has also been known to put stories and puzzles in his manuals in order to explain the material, and he even created a board game once to illustrate a complex process.

As you might imagine, Kevin has very little use for John's tools in particular and for his "dictate-and-run" style (as Kevin calls it) in general. So Kevin also applies his creative talent and boundless energy to gently teasing and joking with John, trying to get him to "come out and play."

JOHN AND KEVIN: DO YOU HAVE THEIR POWER?

Both of the main characters in our opening stories display a talent for creating something new. This power is based on their ability to perceive their environment differently from the "norm." John can see ways in which data might be put together and displayed in order to reveal new aspects or possibilities in a project. Kevin finds unusual (and memorable) ways to help others understand complex topics. In contrast to a Builder, who takes what literally exists (such as a project-management tool or a manual) and enhances its functionality and efficiency through known "laws," John and Kevin look for new (even metaphorical) configurations and connections that create new realities (such as project visioning) or that show new ways of perceiving old realities (such as modems as ferries).

However, John and Kevin aren't equally effective in their creativity. Why not? John's creativity happens in a vacuum. No one else is involved until the "artwork" is complete and ready for viewing. And as you may have noticed, John's "creativity" lies in putting distance between himself and others; he stays in his office, and he all but says that the real beauty of his tool is that it allows him to check on projects without having to talk to anyone ("track you down").

Kevin, on the other hand, constantly expresses his perceptions and ideas in order to get others' reaction. Can they learn from it? Will they use it? Is it an effective and helpful way of looking at something? Kevin wants to be involved, and wants others involved, on more than just an intellectual basis. John wants compliance; Kevin wants "ah-ha's."

In this chapter we'll take a look at the type of personal power that John and Kevin demonstrate, the power of creativity. The more positive and effective manifestation of that power we'll call the Artist; its more isolated and less effective counterpart we'll call the Loner. Let's look first at the personal power of the Artist.

THE POWER OF THE ARTIST

Artists see things differently. And it's not just visual seeing, but perception of all kinds—the five senses, intuition, paying attention to feelings and nuances of behavior (and not just in people). Artists can sense what's happening on many levels, and can represent it in a way that others understand with both head and heart.

However, your first reaction to an Artist (including the one within you) is likely to be, "Where did THAT come from?" Therefore, an important first step as you learn about Artist power is to suspend your judgment about what's being created. (The next chapter on the Judge has some ideas on how to do that.) The second step is to realize that these new, crazy ideas must be shared. An Artist's true power comes from a desire to make something where nothing was before, and share it in the hope that it will inspire others' creativity. The power of Artists lies in their ability to use their own creativity to unleash a cascade of creativity in others. Let's see why Artists are able to do this and how they act in creatively powerful ways.

KEYS TO THE ARTIST'S POWER

The source of the Artist's power comes from two areas:

1. *Artists attend to a very wide range of stimuli.*
   Artists accept almost anything as valid sensory input. This allows them to perceive connections that others miss. To use the popular jargon, Artists are masters of the "interface"; they perceive (and feel) how details affect behavior. And Artists feel connected to what they're perceiving. They internalize rather than just observe, which allows them to touch the core or essence of something and use it in their own work. (You can see this in actors who, by keenly attending to the nuances of behavior, convincingly "become" the person they're playing. Tom Hanks's portrayal of a child in *Big* is a good example of the power of the Artist to perceive details and connections and to create something delightfully new.)

2. *Artists don't make assumptions about how things should be used or how they should fit together.*
   Although Artists attend to a plethora of input, they do so nonjudgmentally, or at least without leaping to conclusions about the natural state of things. Kevin can create useful analogies that enhance learning (and will be remembered long after the fact) because he doesn't assume that ferries and modems have nothing to do with each other. He's able to see that they both carry things (electrons and people) and that the familiar might be used to explain the unfamiliar. He also doesn't accept that manuals and parlor games belong on separate pieces of "canvas." They both can explain a process or strategy, so he puts them together and creates a new approach to understanding technology.

In short, Artists' power stems from their ability to sense deeply and broadly, and present their experience in new and different ways that will awaken others to new possibilities. (We emphasize "new and different" as a cornerstone to the power of the Artist because theirs is often the only type of power that can jolt people out of habitual ways of perceiving.) We can sum up the Artist's personal power this way:

Artists choose a way of personal power that creatively communicates what they're perceiving, and changes the perceptions of others in the process.

TWELVE CHARACTERISTICS OF ARTIST POWER

Now that we've seen the underpinnings of an Artist's power, let's take a look at the behaviors by which an Artist effectively exercises that power:

1. *Artists present drafts for feedback and comment.*

   It's important to Artists that the object and the experience are calibrated (i.e., that you'll interact with their work in the way they intended). So they test out their ideas on a regular basis and incorporate feedback (perhaps in unusual ways) into subsequent work.

   Example: Arthur, a space planner, has drawn the work area for a new office building based on what the owner said she wanted and some new ideas that Arthur has about how to encourage group interaction without creating too much noise. He knows it's important for the client to see her own requirements in the floor plan, but he'd like her to consider his ideas, too. So Arthur presents several drafts that incorporate both their ideas in various degrees. The client says she wants more open space.

2. *Artists fantasize out loud.*

   Artists can see a plethora of possibilities, and they try them all out under the assumption that something's bound to work (i.e., give them new insight).

Example: The client wants more open space, so Arthur talks with her about having people work at home on alternate days so the office workers will have more room; having "white noise" in some areas to increase the (aural) space; about using light colors instead of dark ones; putting all employees (not just managers) in offices; putting all employees (including managers) in one big open area with no walls and plenty of plants; having games and novels around to give some psychological space from work. The client tells Arthur to "get real."

3. *Artists pay as much attention to the artistic process as to the artwork itself.*

Artists understand what it takes to be creative. They deliberately set up their environment to help them see things in new ways.

Example: Arthur sees that he's made a serious mistake. He's always brought his ideas to his client's office—hardly the place for inspiring creativity in either of them. So Arthur takes his client to the local art museum, which has implemented some of the space ideas that Arthur suggested earlier. (In other words, he's working on the process of creativity that he and his client share, and not just on the outcome.) The client likes the museum but wonders if the approach will fit in with the "culture" of her organization.

4. *Artists participate.*

Artists know that from masses of input come sparks of insight. They engage and observe in order to perceive and feel what's going on and to catch the moment when new possibilities present themselves.

Example: Arthur moves into his client's organization for a while, working with the group, eating with them, and relaxing with some of them after work. This is definitely a button-down office, and the group doesn't "play" much at work. Arthur sees why some of his earlier ideas may not be accepted. On the other hand. . . .

5. *Artists can work within the group's rules in unusual ways.*
Artists who effectively employ their power can accept the charter of the group without blindly accepting all of its norms for what constitutes "good work." True Artists can delight and surprise their customers and still give them what they want.

   Example: Arthur accepts that it's very important to the group that they look professional to their own customers, and that they not "goof off." However, they could loosen up and communicate a bit more, which is where their boss was going with her open-space idea. At the end of his stay with the group, Arthur suggests that perhaps they could create a "false front" to their work area: a place with four walls, desks, and chairs, where the group would work with customers. Behind that, though, they'd have a real work area with movable walls, "undefined" areas that could be configured according to the task, offices for privacy, etc.

6. *Artists make time to be inactive and to reflect.*
Artists know they need to replenish their creative energy. They deliberately take time to do nothing, trusting that deep internal processing will continue and give them new insights.

   Example: Everyone wants some time to think about Arthur's proposal and about how they might do work differently. Arthur welcomes the break and spends a few days walking on the beach and playing his piano. He's been on "sensory overload" lately, and he can just now feel his brain begin to clear.

7. *Artists give in to creative concentration.*
Artists (unlike Loners, whom we'll meet later on) don't deliberately withdraw from society, but they do realize that the creative

urge may require them to "clear the decks" of any other plans and commitments for a while.

Example: In an instant, Arthur clearly sees how the workspace will look. Knowing what's coming, he surrounds himself with food and drink, gets into comfortable clothes, turns off the phone, and spends several hours allowing the picture to flow unimpeded from his mind, through his hands, and onto the drafting table.

8. *Artists revise their work, but they also know when it's "done."*
Remember that Artists want to share their unusual perceptions in the hope that others will be inspired to see differently also. To that end, Artists will modify their work to make it more "accessible," but they'll stop short of making it just what you expected (since that wouldn't make you see in a different way).

Example: Arthur bows to the group's wish to have their manager in a permanent office; however, in the final plan he retains the idea of having some unassigned offices that can be used by anyone who needs private space.

9. *Artists give others room to interpret their work.*
Artists tend to install or implement their work initially without a great deal of explanation or interpretation. They know that part of inspiring creativity in others is seeing what new ideas they'll bring to your work.

Example: Arthur and the group are there as the new office space is built. Arthur doesn't say much, but he does suggest ways in which items usually relegated to the background (such as plants and lights) might help the group make effective use of the open space.

10. *Artists delight in creating "ah-ha's."*
Artists really don't care if others judge their work by some artistic standard. What they want most is evidence that they've made an intellectual and emotional connection to their audience that

makes the latter gasp at the new insights and wonder at all the new possibilities.

Example: Arthur is there when the new office space is ready. Although the group has seen the area before, this is the first day they'll work there. Arthur enjoys the little surprises that come all day long as workers discover what they can do with the new space, what they can do that they didn't think they could before now.

11. *Artists create connoisseurs, not just users.*
    Because of their attention to the underlying connections, Artists can create an understanding of fundamental concepts or values beyond their individual pieces of artwork. This understanding allows Artists (and others) to use their creativity in new situations where the same fundamentals still apply.

    Example: Arthur's creativity with the physical environment showed his client and her group that openness was a key value for them, regardless of the "button-down" nature of their environment. They have begun to apply the Artistic power that they tapped while arranging the walls and furniture to other aspects of their work. Arthur hears the group talking about creating an "organization without walls," that is, one in which hierarchy and job specialization are less rigid.

12. *Artists play.*
    Artists know that in silliness and mindful abandon they just might perceive something in a new light or catch a glimpse of a new connection.

    Example: At the end of the project, Arthur takes one of his original drawings, tears it into random pieces, and blows them into the air. One lands on his coffee cup and another on the floor, which causes him to wonder about creating the same space on different levels. Suppose he puts in some stairs and creates lofts instead of private offices. . . .

THE ARTIST IN THE WORKPLACE

Given the characteristics of the Artist that we've just described, how do they make a contribution to an organization? Because of their ability to see almost everything from a different perspective, Artists can get organizations out of ruts and away from group-think. In addition, since Artists pay attention to how people feel about and *relate* to something, as well as how they *think* about it, Artists can advise on the "human" part of the business equation. They'll understand immediately why logically creative systems (such as John's) fail in the human context. As we mentioned earlier, the Artist has a superb understanding of the interface (in its broadest connotation) that must be created so that work can get done.

THE ARTIST'S RELATIONSHIP WITH OTHER TYPES

If you are an Artist, or if you have Artists in your organization, you'll find an especially productive relationship between this type and Shamans or Sages. Shamans have powers of perception beyond those of the Artist, and the latter will appreciate and enjoy working with someone who can see even further. For their part, Shamans and Sages both need Artists to translate their often esoteric visions and paths into more accessible forms (such as pictures or poems or models).

As you might imagine, Artists have trouble working with the power types who tell you what to do or how to think and perceive (such as Controllers). Also, despite the popular image of Artists as nonconformists, the Artists we've described here won't have much patience with Rebels (who waste their creativity by going their own way rather than by creating a new way).

PROBLEMS OF THE ARTIST

The power to perceive differently and express yourself creatively can lead to three problems you should watch out for if you're trying to develop the Artist within you:

- *Because Artists accept so much sensory input, they can overload and shut down.*
  Make sure you give yourself permission to rest and reflect. Doing nothing is a crucial "activity" for Artists; it gives your input buffers a chance to empty out and process your perceptions and impressions.
- *Artists naturally want to create—even when it's not practical to keep doing so.*
  You'll need to pay attention to the organizational and interpersonal clues that tell you when it's time to stop creating new things and start using what you have.
- *Artists need to watch their tendency to use their power to creatively thwart plans and people they don't like (especially those who work "by the book"—a style that's anathema to the Artist).*
  Be careful about venting your creative energy in black humor and cynicism; both will isolate you from relationships that you need to fuel your artistic power.

The powerful lesson of Artists is that they succeed not so much because they do something completely new but because they perceive the mundane differently and see possibilities where others haven't looked. Their different perspective can be enormously useful to other artists, as well as to laypeople, because they share their ideas and their processes and invite participation in the adventure.

There is, of course, a way to be creative and not share it. We don't think this use of your personal power will help you in your life and work; however, we'll present it as an illustration of where you need to be careful in developing your own Artist. Let's take a look at this misuse of creative power in the character of the Loner.

THE LONER (THE ARTIST'S ALTER EGO)

As we saw in the opening story about John, the creative power of the Artist can be applied so that it results in isolation, which is exactly what the Loner wants. Does that make a Loner personally powerful? We don't think so, but Loners can certainly *look* powerful, because when they come out of their shells to get what they want, they often do it in a very creative and aggressive way that's hard to resist. Let's examine why that is.

THE LONER'S CREATIVE POWER

Loners seem to be creative for two reasons. First, they tend to appear with finished work in hand, which they then offer to you. Here's where the problem starts: Since you aren't privy to the Loner's plans, it's easy to assume that the Loner must be a genius who can just come up with a finished solution. If you can't see the brilliance of the gift, then you're the one with the problem—an attitude that gives the Loner tremendous power over you.

Second, Loners seem creative because they often take a leadership or teaching role in explaining the newness and importance of their work to others. This public display misleads you into thinking that Loners are presenting the fruits of their creativity for the general good, instead of as a way to get them what they want most: to be left alone. Adept Loners use their creativity to prevent you from seeing that their genius has actually been applied to creating something that protects their isolation.

Loners don't want to share their art; they want you to be so busy trying to make sense of it that you'll leave them alone. John didn't want to share his new ideas on project management. What he really wanted was to keep tabs on his team's projects without having to leave his office and talk with them.

Is this isolationist behavior powerful? Unlike the Artist, who periodically (and consciously) chooses isolation in order to let the creative fever run its course, the Loner just wants to hide. Loners will argue that they can get others' ideas without interacting, or that their own ideas are creative enough. And on the rare occasions when Loners do interact, they look powerful because they act creatively and persuasively to get what they need. Yet even reclusive Artists know that their real creativity (and hence their real power) only comes from sharing their perspective with others and participating in the cross-fertilization of ideas. Loners spend their power avoiding both.

THE LONER IN THE WORKPLACE

Because Loners use their power to create self-isolation, you often won't know what Loners are doing or how they add value to the organization. Despite the creativity of their ideas, Loners usually have great difficulty getting support for their projects because they haven't made known their plans and ideas along the way. In short, Loners haven't figured out that others don't like surprises and don't like to be presented with completed "gifts" whose logic and use they then have to discover.

As organizations "right-size" and downsize, Loners are apt to be the ones who are laid off, since no one knows about their contributions or creative potential. Even in better times, Loners, by their self-imposed isolation, still miss out on the joys and rewards of sharing others' delight in a new way of perceiving or in a new idea that helps them see possibilities for doing work in a way that brings out the creativity in everyone.

ARTISTS AND LONERS:
ESSENTIAL DIFFERENCES

As we've seen, Artists and Loners both have the power of creativity. Why is one more effective than the other in using personal power? The answer lies in three fundamental differences in how Artists and Loners view energy, depth, and distance:

1. Artists draw energy from the things around them and the ideas, behaviors, and simple presence of the people around them. They're fueled by connection and interaction. Loners, on the other hand, are terrified of having their energy drained away by people who always demand too much of their creative power. (Things, but not people, usually are safe for the Loner.)

2. Loners are afraid of what they might discover if they look deeply into anyone (including themselves). There might be some ugliness in the depths. Worse, they might open themselves up to challenge and criticism, a risk that just isn't worth it to a Loner. So, as we saw with John, Loners employ their creative power to stay isolated, keeping their relationships at a surface level only. Artists, on the other hand, willingly plumb the depths. They see any discovery (even an ugly or frightening or hurtful one) as something new that might enhance their own creativity. (It's been said especially of musicians—from Beethoven to Fleetwood Mac—that they are most creative in their deepest, darkest moments.)

3. Artists use distance sparingly and consciously to give their creative power room to roam. They may disappear, but not for long. And

they return with fresh insights and a burst of energy for re-establishing relationships. In contrast, Loners actively create distance from anything that might suck their energy or draw them in too deeply.

These underlying differences influence how Artists and Loners behave when they use their power. The box on page 142 summarizes the differences in how Artists and Loners act on their creative power.

Essential Differences Between Artists and Loners

Artists . . .	Loners . . .
• present drafts	• present "completed" work
• talk about the (plethora of) directions they'd like to explore	• share plans reluctantly and with few details
• consider the artistic processes as important as the "work of art"	• expect rewards for the ends they achieve, regardless of the means
• engage as participant-observers	• participate in the group as leaders or teachers, but not as members
• approach the group's charter and goals in unusual ways	• persistently pursue opportunities outside the group's charter or goals
• rest and reflect	• keep themselves and others busy
• take refuge in creative concentration	• take refuge in illness
• modify their "artwork" to make it more accessible (yet know when to stop making changes)	• grudgingly make modifications so that (less competent) others can use their work
• give others the space (or hints) to interpret their work	• sit back (or leave) as others struggle to implement their work
• want "ah-ha's"	• want obedience
• create connoisseurs	• create adversaries
• play	• hide

Now that you've seen the characteristics of creative power, let's take a look at some actions you can take to develop the Artist (and curtail the Loner) within you.

Bringing Out the Artist in You: A Checklist

Here are our suggestions for enhancing the Artist within you and in your organization:

✔ *Don't be afraid to present work-in-progress.*

The Artist takes her sketches for the new library to the people reading in the library.

The Loner has his blueprints sent to the city planning commission.

✔ *Put your half-baked, crazy ideas out there.*

The Artist talks about a gym in the library—read while you work out.

The Loner is vague about the colors and fabrics for the reading room furniture, and resents your question as an attack on his competence.

✔ *Find out how (not just what) you create.*

The Artist notices that she went to the users (the readers) before she went to the staff with her ideas, perhaps not wanting the "wet blanket" of "This is how we do things here."

The Loner wants you to appreciate the unique look and genuine comfort of the reading room (despite the fact that the furniture had to be taken apart to fit through the door).

✔ *Practice being involved and observing at the same time.*

The Artist spends time in the library to see how she and others use (and "misuse") the space.

The Loner presents a seminar to the library staff (but not at the library) on the latest design of stacks and administrative areas.

✔ *Don't fight the goals (unless they're really out of whack), but find creative ways to meet them.*

The Artist works to design an environment that makes reading deliciously comfortable by providing space to sit, stand, lie down, and walk around with books.

The Loner designs a space that can be used for meetings, research, writing, preparation of multimedia presentations, and other activities that might come to mind later. (That some of these might not be compatible with quiet reading is a problem for the users, not the Loner, to solve for themselves.)

✔ *Take a break and clear your mind.*

The Artist puts her designs aside and takes a walk.

The Loner gives assignments to the library staff so they won't call him while he's trying to get work done.

✔ *When the creative urge hits, surrender to it without feeling guilty.*

The Artist puts out the "Closed" sign on her studio on the day that the library design becomes clear in her brain. (By that afternoon, she's open for business again, having transferred the whole design to one page in a frenzy of creative activity.)

The Loner discovers he has Attention Deficit Disorder, which will prevent him from working in the distracting atmosphere of the library, with all those people. He'll do the designs in his office instead, and leave messages for the library staff if he needs anything. (This isn't as far-fetched as it sounds. We actually know a Loner manager who, after much research, discovered that he had ADD. Although ADD is a legitimate disorder, we believe in this case that the manager exploited it beyond its real effect on him in order to avoid interactions with others.)

✔ *Be willing to make some changes so that others can relate to your work, but stop before it begins to look like everyone else's.*

The Artist, at the request of the staff, modifies her plans for bed-like couches (for those who want to lie down to read), but leaves in the beanbag chairs (which could be used for the same purpose).

The Loner grudgingly withdraws his plans for the meeting rooms and multimedia systems so that "the masses" can read in peace.

✔ *Sit still and be quiet while others absorb your work.*

The Artist is present (but quiet) while the staff members
have their first experience with the movable stacks she's designed. She's about to hint that such stacks might allow the staff or the readers to configure the library's space in new ways.

The Loner watches for a few seconds, then steps in to demonstrate (with a rather arrogant approach that clearly communicates "You could figure out my elegant design if you'd just think about it").

✔ *Rejoice in "ah-ha's."*

The Artist is delighted when the staff beats her to the punch and figures out three different ways to use the movable stacks before she can give them any hints.

The Loner insists that the staff use the movable stacks as he intended—for special exhibits of rare books that can be looked at but not touched.

✔ *Help others understand why your work speaks to them, and how they can find that connection in other (seemingly unrelated) works.*

The Artist has created a cadre of connoisseurs of "quiet space" who are now looking at their homes and other venues as places where such space might be created.

The Loner has succeeded in pitting the staff against the public in a fight for the "best" use of the library's space. He can get some peace and quiet for himself while they fight it out.

✔ *Play for the joy of discovery.*

The Artist imagines libraries in unusual places (like restaurants), and makes a game of discovering the quietest spots in her favorite eateries.

The Loner goes home so that he won't have to attend the library staff's TGIF party and listen to any more of their ideas.

SUMMING IT UP: THE POWER OF THE ARTIST WITHIN YOU

Of all the power types we describe in this book, the personal power of the Artist may be buried deepest within you. What you had to do to get where you are (do well in school, please the boss, etc.) probably caused you to distrust perceptions that didn't match the norm and suppress the creative urges that those perceptions inspired. Yet it is the power of the Artist that will make you employable in ways that fulfill you and your organization in the long run. Peter Senge has said that the ability to learn may be the only sustainable competitive advantage; if so, then the Artist within you is best suited to help you learn, since he or she can perceive and appreciate a rich variety of stimuli. To turn this learning into creative outputs, remember the following keys to Artist power:

- Stay open and available to new inputs and ideas, even if they're uncomfortable.
- Put as many ideas out there as you can, even if they're half-baked. Something is bound to stick and cause others to see things in the new light you created.
- Most importantly, allow your creative power to flow. Don't block it by trying to be Superperson (which only means that you drive very skillfully in the rut). Do nothing, and watch how new connections and possibilities paint themselves on your canvas.

PERSONAL POWER STRATEGY #6

RELEASING THE JUDGE WITHIN

Having gone to bed well after midnight, an instructor stumbles into work just minutes before he's due to start teaching a management-skills class. His co-trainer, Sherri, pokes her head over the cubicle wall, saying, "Why do you do this to me? I can't teach this class by myself!" (And thinking, "My ratings are going to be bad because of you.")

✳ ✳ ✳

One of Jonathan's colleagues has been absent from several recent meetings where her reports are needed to keep a project on track. As the result of the missing reports, a crucial deadline has come and gone, delaying the project. Jonathan starts a conversation with his *colleague by saying, "I'm worried about you—it's not like you to miss meetings. As you know, we need your reports to keep the project on track. I'd like to understand the problem and see what I can do to help."*

✳   ✳   ✳

Sherri and Jonathan deal with their situations quite differently. Sherri judges her colleague harshly and goes on to upbraid him in a pattern that renders both of them powerless. Jonathan, on the other hand, brings his judgment to bear in a positive and helpful way. In this chapter, we'll take a look at how Jonathan exemplifies the Judge, while Sherri takes the role of the Preacher.

Perhaps more than any other type, the Judge (and its alter ego, the Preacher) wields tremendous power to build up (or tear down) your own sense of empowerment. Critics (both external and internal) can help or threaten your self-esteem and competence, the twin keys to your own power base. In today's turbulent and uncertain work-places, the power to judge can provide a set of coherent standards by which you can assess behavior and confidently know what to do next, while the power to criticize can define you (and others around you) as incompetent. Most people display a mixture of the Judge and the Preacher. They find that their Judge and Preacher battle ten rounds every day as they fight to convince themselves that they are (or are not) worthwhile people. In such cases, the Preacher wins by a knock-out.

SHERRI OR JONATHAN: WHICH ARE YOU?

You may already begin to see some of Sherri or Jonathan in yourself. Each embodies some key characteristics of a type of power that comes from judgment. We call the more negative manifestation of that power the Preacher; the more positive (and effective) one we call the Judge.

The Preacher:

- loves to make snap judgments
- asks a barrage of berating questions (which cannot be answered without self-incrimination)
- ends up feeling helpless (and making others feel incompetent)

The Judge, on the other hand:

- establishes agreed-upon and overt criteria for competence
- asks nonthreatening questions about a situation and shows compassion without condemning behavior
- moves quickly to restore a feeling of competence

Sherri's colleague hears only the voice of accusation, but Jonathan's does not hear any "judgment" from him at all. His colleague knows that he really wants to help her judge her own actions, see their impact, and figure out what to do next.

The Judge and the Preacher are probably working right now in people with whom you work and have relationships. And like most of us, you probably have a "Preacher" within. This internal critic can be harder on you than anyone else and may be holding you back from realizing your Judge power (and other types of power). You can't escape Preachers and critics (internal or external), but you can learn how to increase your own personal power by being more Judge-like and less Preacher-like.

In this chapter we'll take a look at ways to enhance your personal power by bringing out the Judge (and toning down the Preacher) in your life and work. Let's first see how Judges operate and how they exercise personal power both inwardly and outwardly.

THE POWER OF THE JUDGE

On the surface, you may be thinking that the Judge embodies all that you've come to dislike about the so-called "empowerment" movement: someone evaluating you and doing something to you (allegedly) for your own good. Yet as you are bombarded with news of every possible moral dilemma, from human- and animal-rights abuses to the "family values" debate, you probably do feel a need for some moral base. The dilemma is that we all resist the imposition (however gentle) of morality that isn't ours. And these days, those attempts to impose morality seldom do so in a gentle and soft-spoken manner—a problem we'll discuss later, in the section on the Judge's alter ego, the Preacher. Our Judge does not impose morality but offers the positive support that can inspire an individual's sense of right and wrong and enhance personal power and accomplishment.

THREE FUNDAMENTALS OF JUDGE POWER

So what is a Judge? A Judge draws personal power from the ability to:

1. *Distinguish what is contextually effective from what is ineffective.*
   This doesn't mean that Judges change their criteria according to which way the wind blows. Judges don't waffle—although it sure looks like it sometimes, when their need to understand gets in the way of the lynch mob. It also doesn't mean that Judges can't act quickly. It does mean that the *first* thing Judges try to do is understand rather than conclude.
   At the beginning of this chapter, you saw Jonathan engage his colleague in a conversation so that he could understand the situation and then do the right (i.e., effective) thing. However, if the building were burning down and his colleague hadn't called 911, Jonathan's judgment about the situation (not about his colleague) would have resulted in a different and much quicker course of ac-

tion. In that case, the effective thing to do would have been crystal clear—no discussion needed.

2. *Resist the (very natural) temptation to determine right from wrong or good from bad in an abstract and eternal sense.*
A Sage might have the power to do that, but a Judge does not. It follows from number 1 above that a Judge's sense of right and wrong stems from knowledge of what it takes to be personally effective. That is, the Judge values "getting to the bottom of things" and taking each case on its own merits—and then acting accordingly.
In the opening story, Sherri had already concluded that her co-trainer wasn't much good. Did you get the sense that no matter what her colleague did, Sherri was going to find something wrong with it? It's hard to know how to be effective when someone (including the critic within you) is second-guessing you all the time. Real Judges, on the other hand, aren't prejudiced in the true sense of the word—they don't judge the present (or future) based solely on past experience.

3. *Focus on the means rather than the ends.*
From what we've said so far about the Judge, you might be starting to see that *how* you get the result—not the result itself—is the true source of your Judge power. For a Judge, the ends by themselves never justify the means. This doesn't mean that Judges don't care about personal goals, company sales targets, etc. It does mean that Judges invest their efforts in relationships with people that result in goals and targets being met. In other words, to a Judge, getting what you want while driving others away in the process would be "bad" (i.e., ineffective).
We saw this in Jonathan's approach to the missed meetings. He could have demanded that his colleague give him whatever reports she had at that moment, and then taken her off the project (implying that she was an incompetent person who did the wrong thing by not meeting her commitments). Instead, he tried to un-

derstand the situation, hoping he'd be able to get what he needed *and* leave the door open for working with his colleague in the future (implying that she was capable of more effective behavior). He didn't overinterpret the situation, reading more into it than was warranted. His colleague missed a meeting—something she's done only once—and Jonathan left it at that. Sherri, on the other hand, read more into the situation than was actually there. Her colleague, too, had only been late once. Sherri could have offered him some strategies (means) to avoid overextending himself rather than merely berating him for the result.

A COUPLE OF KEYS

At this point you might be saying to yourself, "This is all well and good, but how does it help me with the really tough moral questions that arise in my daily life and work? How can the Judge help me raise my children or accomplish more with my project team at the office?" Consider a couple of keys:

- The issue you see on the surface (helping your kids succeed in school, getting a team to meet an objective on time) isn't the real issue. The real issue is creating a climate where achievement becomes possible.
- A moral stance (a judgment) on a surface issue probably won't result in effective behavior on your part, at least not in the long run. Remember: A Judge's power comes from the ability to get below the surface of what's happening to a "moral core" that makes effective and consistent behavior possible.

So how can you use your personal power to take a stance on moral issues in an effective way? In the next section, we'll describe some specific characteristics of Judges that help them deal with the day-to-day issues as well as with the larger moral issues in their lives.

WHAT DOES JUDGE POWER LOOK LIKE?

Judges are powerful (and they help others see their own power) because they apply their "judging" processes and criteria to themselves and their own behavior first; that is, they constantly engage in self-judgment. They live their lives by examining their goals (to make sure they will really meet their needs), laying out a process that will enable them to reach those goals, and checking periodically to ensure that no one (including themselves) is being damaged by their goals or their methods.

If you're familiar with the ideas of St. Thomas Aquinas, you'll recognize this as his principle of the "well-formed conscience." This means more than being conscientious about one's self. Judges are able to extend their judgment beyond themselves to those around them because they always assess their actions' impact on others. A Judge's conscience is tuned to "we," a Preacher's to "I." In the opening scenarios, Jonathan (the Judge) was thinking about how he and his co-worker could fix the problem together. Sherri was thinking only of the impact on herself.

Let's take a look at specific behaviors that further define the power of the Judge.

NINE CHARACTERISTICS OF THE JUDGE

Judges "get to the bottom of things" and act consistently on that information because they:

1. *Don't judge right away.*
   Judges start from a neutral position. (This is the hardest thing to remember about your own Judge.) A Judge's very first act is to understand, asking "What's going on?" instead of "What should have happened?"

Example: One of your young music students has made no progress on a piano piece he's been practicing for the past two weeks. You (as a Judge) ask, "Can you describe to me how you've been practicing this piece?" He says, "I just play it straight through lots of times."

2. *Focus on the impact of the behavior.*

    After coming to understand the situation, a Judge communicates "judgment" by describing its impact on everyone involved, rather than making a pronouncement about its rightness or wrongness.

    Example: (continuing the piano scenario) You say, "When you just play it straight through, it doesn't give you a chance to stop and work on the hard parts and 'get them into your fingers.'" He says, "I know. But I like the feeling of finishing it—you know, getting to the end and having done it."

3. *Apply a set of agreed-upon values consistently.*

    Note that we said "agreed-upon values." This helps the Judge reinforce consistent behavior. Having taken the time to examine what's important (something that Sherri didn't do), the Judge engages all concerned in a values discussion (rather than assuming that others will naturally accept the Judge's own value system).

    Example: You say, "I know. I like that 'getting done' feeling too. However, when you started taking lessons, you talked about how important it was to you to learn the piano well enough to accompany your friends when they played solos on other instruments. I liked that idea too." He says, "Yeah, that's still important to me."

4. *Ask questions.*

    This is the most important thing a Judge does. Period. There are a plethora of reasons to ask questions: to understand the situation, to find out what you and others are feeling, to discover how you got from A to B, and to look for alternatives and solutions.

Example: You say, "OK. Then how might you practice so that you can be good enough for your friends, and not frustrate yourself in the process?" He says, "I could practice a difficult part a few times and then play the whole piece again." (He tries that. The hard part sounds better, but the transitions to and from it are rough.)

5. *Look for causes and connections.*
Rather than taking the situation at "face value," Judges look beyond the initial details to see how other behaviors or circumstances might affect their understanding of the situation (and its resolution). They also help others get past their own tunnel vision.
   Example: You say, "Does it sound like it fits together?" He says, "No. I can't get it to sound right with the other parts of the piece."

6. *State what they want.*
Having examined the situation, Judges render their judgment in terms of what they want. That is, they don't make a vague appeal to what's right or good; they get specific. They then check out their judgment with others, both to determine if they've understood and to see if they have any other suggestions.
   Example: You say, "Here's something I'd like you to try, then. When you hit a rough spot, stop and practice it just like you did, and then practice it with the measure just before and just after it. Then back up and play the whole piece through that point so you can see what it sounds like when it's all connected. What do you think?" He says, "That's going to take a long time. How about if I do that to just two hard parts each day?" You say, "Great idea!"

7. *Examine their own role in creating the situation.*
Judges look at their own behavior, at their own trail of connections and assumptions that may have caused or contributed to the situation. They also offer to help (as Jonathan did in the opening scenario), even though they aren't "at fault" in the superficial sense.

156

Example: You say, "Let me take another look at the pieces I've given you. Maybe they really are too hard. I'll play them again myself so I can really understand what you're talking about when you say you're having trouble."

8. *Say "I'm wrong."*

   Judges readily admit when they've made an error in judgment. They know that admitting a mistake won't make others think badly of them, and that they will in fact rush to help the Judge get back on track. (This is a subtle but important point about real Judges: They're not automatons who blindly and coldly makes airtight decisions. Most people take great glee when such lofty giants stumble. Our Judge is a human being who sometimes make a mistake, admits it, and asks for help.)

   Example: You say, "I should have looked at these pieces before. I think they are too hard, and I can understand why you're frustrated."

9. *Listen.*

   Judges make sure they've heard and understood what's being said and felt. They're not trying to outshout others in order to triumph over them with their superior sense of what's "right."

   Example: You say, "What do you think?" He says, "Well, I like your idea of practicing the hard parts and the measures around them. Could we try that on an easier piece? Maybe if I get the hang of it there. . . ."

Maybe this doesn't sound like the "judging" you're used to. The difference is that it's stated and acted upon in a way that's different from what you've experienced all your life (negatively and punishingly). Let's face it: Your student's piano playing sounds awful. He just doesn't practice the way he should (the way you want him to), and his playing is an embarrassment to you. What would other students' parents say about your skill as a teacher if they heard him?

Here's the point: Judges have those feelings too. They get irritated when others—or they themselves—don't meet their standards. However, they quickly see that their irritation isn't about the surface issues (how well their student plays the piano). Judges go in search of the root cause (how the student approaches something he wants to do but isn't good at yet). They don't bully someone into seeing it their way. ("Play it like this.") And they don't write someone off because their own expectations weren't met. ("You'll never be as good a pianist as I want you to be.") In short:

Judges have the ability to state their position and act on it without defeating the other person.

THE JUDGE WITHIN

The real Judge within you isn't that loud, persistent, nagging voice that you've been listening to since before you can remember. The Judge within is that place where you can feel (rather than hear) what's right and wrong. You may call it gut instinct, but it's more than that. It's the place you go to check out what's really going on and to find out what you should do. If you doubt this place exists, just watch what happens the next time you're planning to do something that you know doesn't square with your moral base. You'll find yourself avoiding something within, hoping that it doesn't see. We're not talking about guilt. We're talking about knowledge of consistent and inconsistent actions.

THE JUDGE IN THE WORKPLACE

What do Judges look like in an organization? As you know by now, you'll see them spend very little time judging (if by that you mean saying what's right and wrong). They don't usually reach a "verdict" until the very end, when all the data are in. Instead, they spend most of their time gaining an understanding of the context and the possible alternatives. In contrast to the traditional stereotype, empowered Judges are open and rarely have their minds made up ahead of time. But they do have a consistent process for making up their minds and for implementing a solution based on moral criteria.

Let's take an example: A group has succeeded in getting a disruptive employee to leave the department. The conversation between the group and the Judge (who in this case happens to be a supervisor in another part of the same group) goes something like this:

Judge: What were you trying to accomplish?

Group: To get her out of the department.

Judge: How did you do that?

Group: We kept a record of every time she annoyed a customer.

Judge: So she's gone; that's the good news. Is there any bad news in this?

Group: Well, the customers are a lot happier, and we're more relaxed now that we don't have to cover for her all the time. But we do have to hire someone else and get them trained— and she is out of a job.

Judge: Was there a way that she might have been a productive employee while she was here? This probably isn't the last time we'll have someone who doesn't quite fit it, and the hiring process takes so long. . . .

The Judge's moral stance in this case is, "Use the resources you have—don't throw them away"; however, instead of lecturing the group on that point, she makes her judgment clear through a series of questions that:

- clarify what the group really wanted (happy customers, not fewer employees)

- focus on consequences to the group (having to hire someone else)
- mitigate the group's need to punish the difficult employee

Judges aren't interested in punishment. They are interested in helping people see what to do differently or better next time. They're also interested in contributing to the solution. Let's replay Sherri's scenario from the beginning of this selection, this time with her as a Judge:

Having gone to bed well after midnight, an instructor stumbles into work just minutes before he's due to start teaching a management-skills class. His co-trainer, Sherri, pokes her head over the cubicle wall, saying, "Looks like you need a little more time to get ready for class. This is going to be a tough group this morning, and we'll need to be sharp. Can I do anything to help you get ready? How about if we rearrange the teaching order so that I go first. . . ."

This time, Sherri's moral stance (as a Judge) is that she cares about herself, her colleague, and their students. The colleague may have made a mistake either in staying out too late or in scheduling a class that day; however, Sherri focuses the conversation on the potential impact (not being alert in front of a tough class) and on the alternatives, not on whether her co-trainer is good or bad. And unlike the first scenario, in which Sherri laments the damage done to her, in this version she focuses on the "we" and on solving the problem as a team.

PROBLEMS OF THE JUDGE

Even though the Judge is a personally powerful type, there are some "blind spots" that you should be aware of as you develop Judge-like capacities within yourself and in your workplace. As a Judge, you may expect others to have spent time and effort formulating a consistent set of criteria for determining what's most effective—the "well-formed conscience" we mentioned earlier; however, the real world often operates according to very selfish definitions of what's "effective." Your Judge is going to feel defeated sometimes by ever-changing definitions of what's "legal" and "illegal" and by arbitrary or self-serving changes in standards.

For example, a Judge will have a hard time working for a boss who changes the definition of "good work" or "good behavior" according to what yields maximum political advantage for this boss. A similar but more subtle example occurs when your own inner critic hampers the development of your Judge by applying different criteria to your own behavior (when, for example, it criticizes you for staying out late with a friend, but then praises you for the same behavior with your boss).

In each of these situations, the most effective Judge-like action you can take is to speak up and say that you are seeing a different set of rules applied to different situations or people. That will at least get the problem out into the open, but it's going to be uncomfortable, especially if you work in a place where such behavior is perceived as "rocking the boat." (Retaliation against government "whistle-blowers" has provided some vivid examples of this problem.)

In a nutshell, the greatest problem you'll face as a Judge is the temptation to succumb to the pressure to rewrite your own rulebook to fit the ethos of the day (or the boss).

THE JUDGE'S RELATIONSHIP WITH OTHER TYPES

The Judge may have an especially close—or problematic—relationship with the following types:

- *A Judge and a King/Queen can be an incredibly powerful relationship.*
  The King/Queen has the strategic "big picture," and the Judge

has the process and standards for realizing the strategy without leaving a (moral) mess behind. (Not that a King/Queen would consciously leave a mess, but Judges often are better than Kings/Queens at checking for missteps in the details of the situation.) In return, Kings/Queens can help Judges grow by giving them access to the broader context. The King/Queen within you will see where you *can* go with your life; the Judge will decide where you *should* go. Without a King/Queen, a Judge's options might be limited. If you think you are a Judge, finding a King/Queen (either within yourself or in someone else) will help you see more of what's possible.

- *Judges will have an especially difficult time with Gamesters and Shrinks.*

  The ephemeral values of the Gamester (who just wants to beat the odds) will baffle the solid moral stance of the Judge. But it is the Shrink who poses the most danger to a Judge. The Shrink, as a purveyor of damaging information, tells people what they want to hear in return for useful information. The Judge, on the other hand, tells others (or, more correctly, helps them find) information that they need to hear—whether or not it's what they thought they wanted. And it's quite likely that the Shrink will have a larger following than a Judge, especially when fear is the prime motivator.

Now that we've taken a look at the Judge, let's examine the Preacher. This type goes in for quite a bit of judging too, but not in the same helpful and personally powerful way that we saw in the Judge. Since we all have Judges and Preachers to deal with, seeing the whole range of "judging" behavior will help cement the idea of what works and what doesn't as you develop this type of power.

THE PREACHER (THE JUDGE'S ALTER EGO)

Remember Sherri? She blasted a coworker for doing something that might have made Sherri look bad. In short, she judged out of fear and blame. But as you now know, this type of judgment isn't the realm of the Judge. Sherri, instead, is a Preacher. Preachers, like Judges, make evaluations from a moral base; however, the differences end there, for three reasons:

1. Preachers are more interested in bringing you around to their morality than in living by that morality themselves. This gives them power over you, but doesn't give both of you power (which is what a truly powerful person is after, in our definition).

2. Preachers rely on verdicts (their own) to protect themselves against the anxiety of uncertainty. Judges rely on process and criteria.

3. With a Preacher you just get words. With Judges you get consistent action along with the words.

THE PREACHER'S POWER

Is a preacher powerful? Yes and no. A Preacher's "power" comes from an awe-inspiring ability to speak with absolute certainty. Preachers always say anything on their minds that they think you need to hear (and that can be quite a bit). They call their behavior being honest and up-front, expressing themselves and their "true nature" (which can seem pretty powerful if you're not accustomed to speaking up for yourself).

A Preacher's judgment packs a terrible finality. It seems to emanate from a predetermined moral stance in which there is no room to negotiate. Unlike Judges, Preachers don't care about understanding the context—in fact, they're afraid of it, since details might reveal holes in the argument. Preachers also don't act in ways that are consistent with their judgments of others. They may camp out on the moral high ground, but they don't live there (as Judges do).

For all their power, Preachers (like Loners) suffer from a lack of relationships. They may have a few close friends who manage to see through their "honesty." More likely, they have a horde of followers to whom they look powerful because they can do (and get attention for doing) something the followers can't: speak up.

THE PREACHER WITHIN

The Preacher within you is that loud, persistent, nagging voice that you've been listening to since before you can remember. He or she is the inner critic in its worst mode. Preachers suck up your power when you make the two typical responses to their tirades: when you cave in or when you yell back. The guilt and lack of confidence that they cause within you can be overwhelming. You just can't do anything right, and therefore you're a bad person.

It takes considerable effort to ignore that inner voice. We've had success in quieting the inner Preacher by respectfully requesting that it speak as a teacher and guide rather than a critic. We've also simply asked our Preachers to be quiet. So far, both strategies have worked, probably because they came from a position of self-confidence that didn't try to engage the Preacher in battle. Of all the alter egos we describe in this book, the Preacher is the most ingrained (and therefore the hardest to get rid of) because it's the internalized voice of all the people who have criticized you throughout your life. You may need to get some help in order to unlearn the responses that allow Preachers (either internally or externally) to steal your power.

THE PREACHER IN THE WORKPLACE

Unlike a powerful Judge, who hears before judging, Preachers disempower themselves by being poor listeners. They seldom hear what others are thinking or feeling, and when they do, they devalue it by immediately rendering a judgment on it. ("Nah, you shouldn't feel that way, because. . . .") Preachers not only miss out on the creative exchange of ideas in an organization by prejudging everything, but sharply limit both the experiences and the feelings they allow themselves.

Let's replay the conversation we used in the section on "The Judge in the Workplace," with a Preacher this time:

Preacher: What happened to Carol?

Group: We got her out of the department.

Preacher: Great! How did you do that? (The way I wanted you to, I hope.)

Group: We kept a record of every time she pissed off a customer.

Preacher: Geez, no wonder there's so much work backlogged. You haven't been doing anything except trying to get rid of her.

Group: Well, the customers are a lot happier, and we're more relaxed not having to cover for her all the time. But we do have to hire someone else and get them trained . . . and she is out of a job.

Preacher: So what? She was a pain in the neck. (And if the next person isn't any better, the group will get rid of them, too. They understand how I think about hiring and firing.)

JUDGES AND PREACHERS: ESSENTIAL DIFFERENCES

So far in this chapter, we've discussed several overt behavioral differences between Preachers and Judges.

At least two underlying factors account for the differences in Preachers' and Judges' behavior (you can probably think of more):

1. Judges have a good relationship with their own internal critic. They use that voice as a guide and a check, and they aren't afraid of giving advice and counsel back to the critic. Preachers are terrified of their inner critic (because they're so critical themselves, and they don't want all of that abuse heaped on them). The typical verbosity of Preachers is their way of drowning out any competition. The Preacher's need to judge others is an outward reflection of the failing grade that Preachers have internalized for themselves.

2. Judges have a powerful underlying ability to face fear without getting lost in it. Since Judges dwell in a realm where morality is paramount, they are well aware of how frightening the daily assaults on personal morality can be. They open their heart, take a deep breath, analyze the situation into smaller parts, articulate a part of their moral foundation, meditate on the fear feeling itself, etc. You may not see them do this; in especially adept Judges, the action happens automatically and works so fast that you'd never know the person was afraid (they're not hiding it, they're over it). In contrast, Preachers are scared out of their wits by the moral consequences of their inconsistent judgments and their rush to punishment. Preachers are loud because they're afraid, not because they're sure.

We summarize these differences between Judges and Preachers in the box that follows on page 167.

Essential Differences Between Judges and Preachers

Judges . . .	Preachers . . .
• say "Help me understand"	• say "You should have"
• help others understand the impact of their behavior	• punish others for the wrong they did
• apply a set of agreed-upon values consistently	• bring others around to their value system
• ask questions	• make statements
• look for causes and connections	• focus on end results
• explain what they want and check to make sure others understand (and ask if they have other ideas)	• expect others to know their expectations (because they are obvious and rational)
• examine where their own thinking was off (when something fails)	• blame others' poor implementation for the failure of their foolproof plan
• readily say, "I'm wrong" when the situation warrants it (i.e., not in a self-denigrating way)	• admit (some of) their error, but hold the other person responsible for it
• listen	• have the last word

BRINGING OUT THE JUDGE IN YOU: A CHECKLIST

How can you increase your own personal power by enhancing the Judge (and curtailing the Preacher) within you? Here are our suggestions for what you can do to gain the power of the Judge, based on the behaviors listed in the box. We've deliberately left the examples rather ambiguous in terms of whether we're talking about the Judge/Preacher within you or in someone else. In the end, it doesn't matter. You grow your own personal power from within, but the specific situations through which you learn can come from inside or out.

- The next time you find yourself rushing to judgment, stop and ask the questions that will help you understand what happened. If you proceed in a situation that you don't understand, two things will happen. First, you'll have to clear up a bigger mess than you started with. Second, a Preacher will seize a golden opportunity to berate you for being so blind, unthinking, etc. One of the biggest favors you can do for yourself is to slow down and really get inside the situation, rather than automatically responding with the set of behaviors that you've always used.

✔ *A critical file has been deleted from the project database.*
   The Judge asks about what has happened.
   The Preacher blames someone for killing the project.

✔ *Describe the impact of the behavior and find out what the intent was. Let go of the (very strong) urge to cause those responsible as much pain as they have caused you (that's the punishment part). A powerful way to do this is to simply acknowledge out loud that you're hurt by what they did (that's the impact part). Asking about their intent will help you understand the situation and will stop them in their tracks in the (very unlikely) event that they were deliberately being "bad."*

The Judge states that the loss of the file will probably delay the project for a week, and asks why the file was deleted.

The Preacher suspects that whoever deleted the file did it on purpose in order to make the Preacher look like a poor project manager.

✔ *State your value position (without trying to convert the other person to it). Be explicit about what's important to you. Don't hide behind what the company or Granma needs—talk about what's valuable to you.*

The Judge states that it's important to her that the project be completed on time.

The Preacher argues that if everyone else cared about the project as he does, things like this wouldn't happen.

✔ *Ask questions. Let's face it: Whoever you're dealing with (even if it's yourself) is expecting a judgment and is cringing at the thought of it. You can take down their (your) anxiety by staying in question mode as long as possible. You may uncover a fact that changes the whole picture.*

The Judge asks for additional information from others in the group—and discovers that the file was deleted locally because the original had been sent to headquarters.

The Preacher makes the "guilty" employee recreate the file.

✔ *Look for causes and connections. You'll find these if you've probed for more facts and details. Looking hard for causes and connections ensures that your judgment addresses a root cause and not a superficial result.*

The Judge realizes that there isn't a procedure for notifying the local staff when files have been sent to headquarters.

The Preacher blames headquarters.

✔ *Be specific about what you want next, and check to make sure whoever you're telling has understood. You might also ask them if they have any other suggestions (a very empowering thing to do). Making others a part of the solution is a good way to take the sting out of judgments. It prevents their Preacher from complaining about their lack of progress.*

The Judge specifies the tasks that she thinks need to be done to get the project back on track and then asks others to fill in the holes in her thinking. She ends the meeting by checking to make sure that everyone knows what they're supposed to do next.

The Preacher says, "Just fix it."

✔ *Take a look at where your own thinking or behavior was off track. Understanding your own contribution to the problem, even if it wasn't remotely your "fault," will help you see what to do differently next time.*

The Judge acknowledges that the employee who deleted the file was a junior project manager, whom the Judge left alone for too long without checking in and giving direction.

The Preacher blames the employee, headquarters, etc.

✔ If your judgment was wrong, say so. It's so important to our usual power base that we be right; however, real power comes from admitting mistakes. Others won't think you're bad; they'll think you're human (and they'll probably offer to help you get back on track).

The Judge publicly states that she made a mistake in not checking with headquarters first.

The Preacher owns up to a mistake (maybe), but blames the employees for not keeping him informed.

✔ *Listen, listen, listen. We've said it before and we'll say it again: The most important task of the Judge is to ask questions and then be quiet and let the full answers reveal themselves. Silence is the Judge's best tool and ally. It allows you to get information, and it keeps you from rushing to a judgment that you may regret later.*

The Judge asks about the file, asks for suggestions, makes sure that everyone has a chance to speak, and doesn't interrupt.

The Preacher says what happened and who's to blame, and tells them to fix it.

SUMMING IT UP: THE POWER OF THE JUDGE WITHIN YOU

Despite all the positively powerful characteristics we've just described, the Judge is perhaps the most difficult type to acknowledge within ourselves and others. As morals and values become ever more contentious and politicized, Judges will be hard-pressed to stay neutral while they do their research, ask their questions, and act in a way that's consistent with their value position.

The behaviors we've listed in the box reflect our culture's ambivalence about the Judge. While the items on the left are characteristic of the Judge, some of the items on the right aren't bad (you're saying to yourself). Why shouldn't you make statements or focus on end results—especially when your boss or your inner critic expects such behavior? If you have a good value system that works for you, aren't you morally obligated to try to bring it to others (the unenlightened, the infidel, the new employee)?

Remember that the power of the Judge is a sustained power to act consistently from a moral base. Those right-hand-column behaviors will bring you power temporarily, but they may cause you to expend at least as much power cleaning up in their aftermath. As you learned about the Judge in this chapter, we hope you discovered the following keys that will help you find the Judge within you:

- A Judge may use a few of the behaviors (such as making statements) attributed to the Preacher in the right-hand column of the box, but only after implementing all the left-hand items. (Jonathan asked about his colleague's situation before reminding her of the expectation that her data were needed to keep the project on track.)
- Judges don't bring others to their value system; they bring their value system to others, and they do so directly—through their own behavior—not indirectly—through words. (Sherri could have put a bit more into her own teaching that day so that both she and her co-teacher would do well.)
- A Judge's first and only concern is to implement a well-thought-out (moral) position without defeating the other person. It's this characteristic that most clearly and uniquely differentiates the powerful Judge from the power thief that is the Preacher. (Jonathan's position was to deliver a quality product on time by working with his colleague, not by blaming her and getting her out of the picture.)

PERSONAL POWER STRATEGY #7

RELEASING THE SHAMAN WITHIN

Betsy is a human resources specialist in a hospital. She's affectionately known as "Dr. Bets" by the staff, not because she has a medical degree but because she's so good at listening to people's problems and helping them talk through the issues until they find an answer (or at least come to a better understanding of the problem). Betsy has a way of allowing any conversation to flow from mundane chatter to intellectual ideas to spiritual topics. This makes it easy for her colleagues to bring up a problem in any of those areas. (Occasionally Betsy brings up her own problem, in which case her colleagues try to be a good "ear" for her.) Betsy is also good at getting a group together to explore a problem in a casual and nonthreatening way. Her interest clearly lies in nurturing healthy and productive relationships among the staff, and she always stays with them while they work through whatever's keeping them from that goal.

✳ ✳ ✳

Linda works with a group of consultants who provide organiza-tional design and management training to small companies. Linda has never forgiven one of the consultants for bragging (in a very innocent way) about his skills during his job interview. To Linda, such behavior just isn't healthy. In response, she sets up a series of mock workshops in which the consultant will have to prove his skills and be "certified." Linda makes it clear that if the consultant doesn't get "better," he may not last long in the department. Linda talks about the consultant's problem with the managers in the group. At the end of the discussion, they not only agree that he needs help but see (thanks to Linda's diagnosis) that all the consultants in the group probably aren't quite up to par and need to go through the certification process. Linda, a consultant herself, should attend the workshops, too; however, she never does. It's clear she thinks she doesn't need them. Although the "sick" consultant goes on to become the most productive member of the team, Linda continues to voice her caution and concerns about his skills. In her estimation, the consultant never becomes fully functional.

BETSY AND LINDA: THE POWER TO HEAL

Do you see Betsy or Linda within you or in your workplace? If so, you are seeing people who use their personal power to bring about health. The difference between Betsy and Linda lies in how they de-fine health; that definition makes them more or less effective in wield-ing their power. To Betsy, health is the ability to function productively in a variety of realms: physical, emotional, spiritual. Linda defines health as others' ability to live up to her standards, which she doesn't believe they'll ever quite be able to do (although she wants to talk with them about it in the hope that they'll see the truth of her diag-nosis and accept her treatment). Both Linda and Betsy want to help others explore their "illnesses," although it's doubtful that Linda really wants others to get well. (She has more power if they're sick.)

In this chapter we'll take a look at the power of Betsy and Linda: the power to heal. We call the more effective user of that power the Shaman; the less effective counterpart is the Shrink.

What Is a Shaman?

Before we describe how a Shaman uses his or her power to effect healing, we should define what a Shaman is and why we chose that name for this power type.

"Shaman" is a term that you've probably heard in an anthropological context; societies that don't have doctors usually have healers who take care of a wide range of illnesses, including, but not limited to, the physical or mental problems that we tend to think of when someone says they're "sick." For example, Rinpoche describes Tibetan Shamans this way:

> *Tibet has its own traditional system of natural medicine, and its own particular understanding of disease. [Shamans] recognize certain disorders that are difficult for medicine alone to cure, so they recommend spiritual practices along with medical treatment. Patients who follow this practice are in many cases healed completely; at the very least they will become more receptive to the treatment they are being given.* (The Tibetan Book of Living and Dying, p. 393.)

What a Shaman in any society really focuses on isn't illness but restoring relationships—bringing people back into the community or back into balance with themselves and their families. It isn't necessary that Shamans find what you might think of as the "real" (i.e., physical) cause of the illness (which is why Rinpoche says that spiritual practice alone often effects a cure); what is important is that patients

175

acknowledge their problems and work through them, often with the help of the Shaman and the community.

Because of this broader definition of sickness and health, one that includes spiritual and emotional issues, we elected not to call the positive power type the Doctor or even the Healer. The first term limits us to the stereotype of the practitioner of Western medicine, who deals mostly with physical problems or mental problems with a physical cause. Neither is the focus of this chapter, since we're dealing with your power in your job and organization. This usually doesn't involve the physical aspects of taking care of your career, but it does involve your power to help yourself and your "community" (organization) stay healthy in emotional and spiritual ways.

In addition, the terms Doctor and Healer imply that you don't use this power unless you're sick, and that you are doing most of the work to find and deliver a cure. The term Shaman, on the other hand, connotes more of a spiritual traveler or a researcher, someone who knows that drugs and surgery aren't the only medicines that work. In addition, Shamans actively involve their patients and other members of the community in any treatment, and maintain a relationship with patients even when they are healthy.

Let's now take a look at how this concept of the Shaman translates into the power to heal that is within you.

THE POWER OF THE SHAMAN

Shamans have the ability to identify and state the nature and cause of illness. Their power stems from their realization that simply owning up to an illness is the first and most important step in taking away the fright and helplessness of being sick. A Shaman helps others to heal relationships and release their creative power. If you feel blocked or hung-up in your ability to realize whichever of the other power types is yours, a Shaman can help you to get past it, to get well by drawing a cure from within.

To do this, Shamans always involve patients and their "organization" in the cure. (Sometimes it's all or part of the organization that is sick; therefore, everyone is involved in the cure, not just the manager or a task force.) Shamans know that it's crucial to involve others in the act of recovering personal power, since that power most often is expressed in relationships at work or elsewhere. Shamans, like Judges, bring illness to light in nonjudgmental ways, and they will see to it that others who are helping you to get well aren't looking for blame (either in themselves or in you) for the illness.

How do Shamans do this? Let's take a look at some of the underpinnings of their power, followed by some specific characteristics and examples.

FUNDAMENTALS OF SHAMAN POWER

A Shaman such as Betsy is able to reach forth and help others who are suffering; that is, those who are not being as effective as they might be in a variety of realms (emotional, spiritual). There are several reasons that a Shaman is able to exercise his or her power, and we'll describe them in a moment; however, one of the major keys is the way a Shaman defines health. Let's take a look at that first.

A SHAMAN'S DEFINITION OF HEALTH

To a Shaman, health doesn't necessarily mean the absence of pain. Many people who live with physical pain or with the pain caused by loss of a loved one function quite well in their jobs and relationships. A Shaman would say these people are healthy; they aren't denying their pain, and they are working through it or with it in a productive fashion. However, when pain prevents people from functioning in known areas of competence, then a Shaman would say they are suffering; that is, they are letting pain get to them in a way that makes them unable to participate.

This difference between pain and suffering is crucial to understanding the power of the Shaman. Let's look at a couple of examples before we go on to the other keys to a Shaman's power:

Rosemary recently lost one of her closest colleagues at work to AIDS. When the pain in her heart became too much, Rosemary found herself withdrawing and becoming preoccupied with her friend's death; she also started getting headaches and losing sleep. So she sought out a trusted friend (a Shaman) who had also known the deceased. This friend helped Rosemary see that her friend's death was bringing up Rosemary's fears of abandonment (the emotional realm) and concerns about life after death (the spiritual realm). The Shaman suggested that Rosemary talk about her colleague to others—about what he had meant to her and what she liked (and didn't like) about him. Rosemary found that others were more than willing to listen, and the more she involved them in her healing, the easier the burden became. Rosemary is still in pain, but her Shaman sees that she's being productive at work and in relationships again.

✳   ✳   ✳

Ken likes to be by himself. He feels nervous around others, but usually he's able to tolerate and even enjoy large meetings and parties because he knows they'll be over soon. Lately, however, Ken has begun to resist interacting with his coworkers and his manager. It seems they're always criticizing him, and he's beginning to interpret everything they say as an indicator that he's done something wrong. Ken lives in fear of the next phone call or piece of mail; it'll probably contain yet another reference to something he's done wrong. Ken's manager (a Shaman) has tried to find a way to create a nonthreatening environment for Ken to talk about what's bothering him, to no avail. Ken is suffering in his isolation but is rather beginning to enjoy it, in a dark and depressed sort of way.

A Shaman would say that Rosemary is healthy and Ken isn't. Although they're both in pain, only Ken is suffering. A Shaman can use his or her power with Rosemary but will have a tough time with Ken, for reasons that we'll explore later on when we talk about the problems of a Shaman. For now, let's look at the other keys to the Shaman's power to heal.

OTHER KEYS TO A SHAMAN'S POWER

In addition to understanding what health is and is not, Shamans are able to exercise their power because they:

1. *Understand the "self-fulfilling prophecy."*
   Shamans believe that people can be well, and they inspire that belief in their patients. This is the Pygmalion effect (named after a king and sculptor who believed his statue, Galatea, was alive, and thus made her so) that researchers have documented in classrooms and workplaces for decades: Believing that someone is good or smart or healthy often makes them so.

2. *Value the spiritual and emotional aspects of health.*
   Since Shamans know that belief can heal, they also know that there's more than just a physical basis to health. Shamans don't discount the physical, but they don't see it as the sole determiner of wellness. Especially since there are many medical professionals (as in your company's health plan) to take care of the physical, a Shaman like Betsy is most likely to concentrate on looking after the emotional and maybe even the spiritual aspects of you and your organization.

To sum up the personal power that Shamans wield, we can say that:

> *Shamans choose a way of personal power that allows illness (in its broadest sense) to be acknowledged, demystified, and treated.*

Let's now take a look at specific ways in which Shamans use their power.

EIGHT CHARACTERISTICS OF THE SHAMAN

Shamans use their personal power to bring about healing because they:

1. *Listen to more than your words.*

   Shamans watch your body language and listen to your tone of voice as well as your words. They can pick up on inflections that indicate that something's wrong, even if you're doing your best to hide it.

   Example: Manny noticed that his boss put her chin in her hand and didn't ask any questions during this morning's meeting. She seemed to be paying close attention to the presentations, and she made decisions with her usual confidence. The others in the room didn't appear to notice anything unusual, but to Manny it looked like his boss just wanted to get the meeting over with.

2. *Make it safe to talk about your fears.*

   Shamans invite you to open up, not because they pry but because they wait quietly for the words to come. They don't offer judgments. Most importantly, you know that what you say to a Shaman won't be told to others without your permission.

   Example: On the way back to the office, Manny mentions to his boss that she didn't seem her usual self in the meeting. He doesn't ask any questions, and he doesn't say, "Do you want to talk about it?" He just puts his observations out there nonthreateningly, and then quietly walks on with his boss. She gives Manny a sharp look as if to say, "How did you know?" and then laughs; Manny has always been able to tell when something's bothering her. She tells him she's worried that her sales team won't make their quota for the month, despite what they said in those upbeat presentations this morning.

3. *Stay with you when you're well, too.*
   Shamans can "read" you (number 1 above) and are safe to talk with (number 2) because they are a part of your life even when you don't need their healing help.

   Example: Manny and his boss haven't worked with each other for very long; however, the boss has found that she and Manny can talk not only about work but about their individual jobs, their families and vacations, and their problems and worries.

4. *Look for cures you will understand.*
   Shamans don't tell you what they'd do or what they think is best for you; they help you identify a cure that's meaningful for you. Shamans know that often you already know what that cure is, but you need some prompting to think of it since you're distracted or afraid (both of which keep you sick).

   Example: Manny knows his boss likes numbers and takes comfort in seeing them, even if they don't tell a positive story. However, before he makes any suggestions, he asks her, "What would make you feel like you had a handle on how the sales are really going?" The boss visibly pulls herself together and tries to think. Manny has used this tactic on her before, and she appreciates that he didn't just tell her not to worry. She says, "It'd help if I could see all of the sales-activity printouts."

5. *Bring others into the healing process.*
   Since Shamans apply their power most of all to healing relationships, they know they can't just give the medicine to you alone.

   Example: Manny is concerned that his boss's discomfort with the sales figures might lead to a situation in which she'll feel that she can't trust her staff, and they'll get defensive when she starts asking for the printouts. Manny voices his concern to his boss. She agrees. He suggests that she call the staff together to work on the problem she perceives (rather than starting with her conclusion that they're going to miss the quota). Maybe the numbers are wrong, or maybe no one (including the boss) is interpreting them correctly.

6. *Heal themselves.*

   Shamans take care of their own health. They know that physical, emotional, and spiritual distractions will keep them from using their power to its fullest.

   Example: Manny's boss asks him to facilitate the problem-solving meeting. She needs to be a participant instead of a leader in this case, and she knows she can't do both at once. Manny notices that her request causes him to feel momentarily irritated; he just can't take one more meeting today! Rather than make an excuse, Manny tells his boss what he's feeling and why he might not be able to be "on" for the several hours it's going to take to get through the sales data. He asks for time to get through some of his own work and proposes the meeting for the next afternoon.

7. *Stay with you during treatment.*

   Shamans are part of your network of relationships; therefore, they know it's important to stay with you during the cure, since it applies to them too.

   Example: Manny facilitates the entire meeting, keeping an eye out for the trust issues he feared might develop between the boss and her staff. It's rough going in a couple of places, but Manny encourages his boss to confront the trust issues each time. It's a risky move for both of them, but by the end of the meeting Manny notices there's considerably more openness between all members of the staff than ever before.

8. *Want you to be well.*

   Despite the role of Shamans as healers, what they really want is for you to be well, not just for you to have a cure when you're sick.

   Example: Manny and his boss discuss how the meeting went. Manny asks her what she might do now so that she doesn't need to have meetings like that in the future. She replies that she wants to have more meetings like that in which the whole staff looks at the numbers together. If they have the meetings more often and keep the communications flowing, maybe they'll see problems early and avoid the tension and mistrust that happened today.

THE SHAMAN IN THE WORKPLACE

Manny's boss found her Shaman in her own organization. You may be accustomed to finding them in your human resources department or in organizational consulting firms. It's often helpful to bring in someone from outside your group to do the "diagnosis," since such a person is less likely to be swayed by the stories that your group typically uses to explain and treat organizational illness (such as "Marketing/engineering is all screwed up" or "If we put in another manager, things will be better").

However, anyone in your organization who takes a holistic approach to relationships will be able to help you. (To find them, listen for people who ask "What are you feeling?" at least as often as they ask "What are you thinking?") Shamans such as Manny will be helpful to your organization because of their ability to bring illness (and its cause) to light in a nonjudgmental way. They won't look for blame, and they will help you develop and implement a cure.

THE SHAMAN'S RELATIONSHIP
WITH OTHER TYPES

Shamans will be particularly helpful to those positive power types (such as Warriors and Builders) who tend to live in the concrete physical world. Although these types do a prodigious amount of work, their tendency to overwork can cause them to lose perspective (i.e., get sick), wondering if they're doing enough. A Shaman can help those types restore balance by showing them how to appreciate the "softer" aspects of power (emotions, spirituality) that Warriors and Builders may discount.

On the other hand, to a Shaman all the less-effective power types are "sick." Their inability or unwillingness to maintain (healthy) relationships comes from their manipulation of the physical, emotional, and spiritual for their own personal ends. If you are a Shaman, you may have a particularly difficult time with Co-Dependents and Loners. The first will see you as a competitor, since Co-Dependents believe they are best at taking care of others. And Loners protect (whether or not they enjoy) their lack of relationships, which makes any organizational cure difficult.

PROBLEMS OF THE SHAMAN

In addition to having trouble with some of the other power types, Shamans may find their power blocked or diminished by a couple of other problems:

1. Shamans can be defeated by organizations or people who don't want to get well. By this we don't mean people with chronic illnesses, or organizations in depressed markets; we mean hypochondriacal organizations and people—like Ken—who enjoy being sick because it brings them attention, gives them an excuse not to succeed, etc. Since Shamans will recognize this situation sooner or later, they are likely to see the "enjoyment of sickness" as an illness in itself and thus hope to be able to treat it.

2. Like the Artist, who is open to many channels of sensory stimuli, the Shaman too can be overloaded by input. In the Shaman's case, it usually happens because too many people are "sick" or because the Shaman is being overly sensitive to everyone's emotions and is

seeing illness where there isn't any (for example, in heated conversations between two coworkers who in fact both thrive on a good argument as the best way to get work done together).

Shamans use their power to bring about healing so that people and organizations can be productive. Others, however, may use a similar power to impose their own definition of "health" or to limit others' power by making them appear to be sick. This is how Linda uses her power in the story that opens this chapter. Let's now take a look at how the power to heal can be used ineffectively by a type we call the Shrink.

THE SHRINK (THE SHAMAN'S ALTER EGO)

Shrinks, like Shamans, are great listeners, and they, too, want you to get well. The difference lies in what Shrinks do with the information they hear and what they mean by "getting well." Knowledge is power for the Shrink, both in terms of how they get it and what they do with it.

A Shrink is the counselor, father-confessor, "ear," or "shoulder" in an organization; however, unlike Shamans, who are interested in relationships, Shrinks are interested in information that they can trade for personal advancement or attention. In short, Shrinks are gossip-mongers, and they thrive on personal and organizational illness and misfortune.

THE SHRINK'S POWER

Shrinks, like Shamans, often have a powerful "bedside manner" of deep caring and concern that gets you to lower your defenses. Shrinks then carefully ration their store of information to selected individuals, making others come to them for the latest "scoop." In contrast to the Shaman, whose power comes from demystifying a situation, the

Shrink manipulates personal and organizational information to keep others off balance.

In addition to rationing information, Shrinks present an illusion of power by insinuating that only they know how to make you well. Beware, though: In reality, you can never get well in a Shrink's eyes, since the Shrink's power depends on keeping you sick.

THE SHRINK IN THE WORKPLACE

Shrinks have a disarming way of getting people to reveal personal and organizational information under the guise of wanting to "reduce the pain around here." One of their more effective tactics to get you to open up to them is to point out how sick other parts of the organization are. (They usually do this by sharing some tidbit of "inside information.") In addition, they often offer their services as a caring (i.e., healthy) alternative to "management."

Because of these tactics, Shrinks are adept at keeping you and others in your organization feeling less powerful than you might otherwise. They have so much inside information that you come to believe that they must be right. We've found that the most effective way to counteract a Shrink is to get a second opinion. Counter their gossip with data; keep the conversation short and then walk away. The more you talk, the more the Shrink will be able to draw you into a discussion about where and why you're wrong.

SHAMANS AND SHRINKS: ESSENTIAL DIFFERENCES

Shamans and Shrinks both care about health. Shamans define that as maintaining productive relationships; Shrinks define it as something they have that you don't. This leads to two fundamental differences in how Shrinks and Shamans think about illness and healing:

1. To Shrinks, an illness is a weakness, ready to be exploited by those who are stronger (healthier), namely the Shrinks themselves. To Shamans, an illness is an inability to function as you normally do. Shamans, therefore, want to close the wound and return you to your productive state. Shrinks, on the other hand, want to hold the wound open, under the guise of getting more information for their "diagnosis."

2. Shamans believe in the mandate "Physician heal thyself." They constantly monitor their own health, knowing that they are less effective in their own relationships, and therefore less effective in helping you "cure" yours, if they are distracted by some emotional or spiritual suffering. In contrast, the only relationship that interests a Shrink is one in which he or she can obtain information. And the only way to do that is to appear powerful (healthy) all the time. By their own reckoning, Shrinks don't get sick; you are the one who has the problem.

The box on the next page summarizes behavioral differences between the Shaman and the Shrink.

Essential Differences Between Shamans and Shrinks

Shamans . . .	Shrinks . . .
• listen to your symptoms on a variety of levels (physical, emotional, spiritual)	• want to discuss your illness
• get your fears out into the open	• play on your fears
• maintain a relationship with you in sickness and in health	• exploit you while you're sick
• look for cures that are meaningful to the "patient"	• know how to fix you
• involve others in the healing	• talk about your "case" with others
• pay attention to their own health	• won't take their own medicine (because they're never sick)
• stay with you during the treatment	• disappear while the treatment is applied
• help you heal	• keep you sick

BRINGING OUT THE SHAMAN IN YOU: A CHECKLIST

Given the characteristics of the Shaman and the Shrink that you've just read about, how might you develop your own Shaman power? Here are our suggestions for bringing out the Shaman within you and in your organization:

✔ *Pay attention to how others are moving and their tone of voice, not just their words.*

    The Shaman quietly mentions to you that you stopped taking notes and seemed distracted (almost as if you were about to cry) in the meeting.

    The Shrink, "concerned for you as a friend and a colleague," invites you into her cubicle to discuss why you didn't seem "with it" in the meeting.

✔ *Make it safe to talk (by telling a similar story about yourself, for example, and by never repeating what you're told unless you ask first).*

    The Shaman tells you about a recent time when he couldn't keep his mind on his work either, and says, "I'm wondering if that's what you felt" (inviting you to talk).

    The Shrink says, "My advice would be to get over it."

✔ *Visit others when they're well, too.*

    The Shaman and you have had some good conversations before, even when there wasn't anything bothering either of you, so you feel safe in telling him your story.

    The Shrink decides that, for your own good, she'd better take you off of her project team until you get control of yourself.

✔ *Look for cures that are known to your patients. (Don't suggest something that might make their fear or pain worse. Note that saying "It's no big deal" is not an effective cure.)*

The Shaman asks about what you've done in the past to help make yourself feel better. (It turns out that getting together with a couple of colleagues to brainstorm solutions to a problem helps you get unstuck.)

The Shrink decides that what you need is to be around people, so she tells your colleagues that they should "unobtrusively" make sure that you're not alone.

✔ *Involve others who are close to your patients in their treatment.*

The Shaman offers to call a couple of your colleagues (the people you've brainstormed with before) and ask them to come over to listen and see if they can help.

The Shrink, professing deep concern for "our best employee," talks about your slip-up to your colleagues.

✔ *Take a break when you need it.*

The Shaman, after talking with you for a while, mentions that he's becoming distracted by an upcoming meeting for which he needs to prepare. If you'll excuse him for an hour, he'll check back in with you when he's taken care of the meeting.

The Shrink stays in her office, making people come to her. She doesn't need to be out in the public areas; her relationships with everyone are just fine.

✔ *Stay with your patients, if they want you there.*

The Shaman sticks around for the brainstorming session you have with your colleagues.

The Shrink sends others to keep you company but doesn't show up herself.

✔ *Help your patients focus on staying well, not just on being able to cure themselves next time.*

The Shaman talks with you about what you might do in the future to head off those feelings of helplessness before they distract you; although he doesn't mind helping you when you're feeling bad, he'd rather see you well (coping effectively).

The Shrink remembers how you were in that meeting, and watches you closely for signs of a "relapse."

SUMMING IT UP: THE POWER OF THE SHAMAN WITHIN YOU

Illness can be a frightening thing. Often we can only guess at what causes it and choose from a very narrow range of options for curing it. However, through the power of the Shaman you can face sickness in your own life and in your organization, acknowledge the fear that comes with being sick, and work with others to effect a cure. As you develop your own ability to heal, remember the following clues to the power of the Shaman:

- What you're working on is wellness, not illness. Remember the self-fulfilling prophecy: If you focus on and expect health, chances are you'll get it more often than if you focus on illness and getting rid of it.
- Accepting the pain can make it diminish or go away. Sometimes we double the pain by trying to push it away. The more we try to hide it, the more it cries out for attention. Acknowledging that it's there is essential to making it go away.
- Just being there is therapeutic. Healing is about relationships. Don't underestimate the power that your presence lends to reducing fear. And two (or more) heads are better than one when it comes to finding a cure.

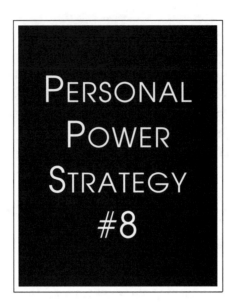

PERSONAL POWER STRATEGY #8

RELEASING THE
SAGE WITHIN

*J*ackie works in a division of the U.S. Government
that moves civilian and military personnel and
materiel around the country and around the
world. That's what he does for a living. What he really does is explore
relationships, not just between people but among all beings, trying to
come to an understanding of the deep interconnections that abound in
the universe. He writes about his experiences and talks about his struggle
to understand emotional, physical, intellectual, and spiritual interconnections. In addition, he helps others to fearlessly look beyond the surface of
their lives.

His coworkers and friends outside work know Jackie as someone
who encourages them to look into and think deeply about themselves and
others. Oddly enough, though, they would never say that Jackie has his
head in the clouds; he's very down-to-earth. They always remark how

present Jackie is when he's talking with them; he's not distracted, nor does he manipulate the conversation for his own objectives. Although he's not an exuberant person, Jackie's friends would all say that he is happy, in a quiet and contemplative way.

IS JACKIE WITHIN YOU?

In this final chapter on the eight personal power types, we're going to describe a type of power that you may read or hear about but may not readily find in your workplace or your personal life. This is the power of deep insight, and we describe it here for some of the same reasons we called out the Aide as a separate type: It's often hidden, it's at odds with many of the acquisitive and spotlight-seeking aspects of our society, and it's incredibly powerful in a quiet and unobtrusive way.

This power of deep insight is the culmination of all of the other power types. It's what Kings and Queens, Artists, Builders, and all the others become when they've transcended their power. Although we haven't implied a progression in the other types, we do believe that the type we'll describe here is a possible "next step" when you've fully realized the personal power of the other effective types. We also believe that even if you don't have this type of power yet, you can use some of its practices to more deeply understand and take advantage of any of the other seven types of power that you do have.

The positive type of this power lives in a person we call the Sage, who practices the power of deep insight in a way that benefits (potentially) all beings. Jackie, for example, uses his power to understand how things and people are interwoven to create a rich tapestry in the present moment, and to understand his own place and work in it. He inspires others not to great external works, perhaps, but to a journey inward to discover their true selves. Perhaps in him you glimpsed some qualities that you have or would like to have: a knowledge of your own depths, a way of seeking without grasping.

In contrast to the preceding seven power types, we'll only be presenting the positive power type—the Sage—in this chapter. We believe that an alter ego (who would use the power of deep insight to get people to happily work and die for a vision) isn't plausible in most workplaces.

A RARE TYPE OF POWER

As you can see, Sages are at the extreme of personal power. Their type doesn't come along very often, although we suspect that there are more Sages out there than we realize. Yet regardless of its apparent scarcity, we believe the power of deep insight is needed to guide all of us in plumbing those depths and understanding those interconnections that will help us to "do the right thing" (in a broad and profoundly thoughtful way) with our own personal power.

Because the power of the Sage is somewhat rare (at least in the organizations and relationships that most of us live in), we don't think workplace examples like those we've used in previous chapters would be plausible to you here. Therefore, in most cases we're going to use real-life people as examples throughout this chapter. We also won't suggest specific behaviors you can try in order to become a Sage, as we have done with all of the other effective power types. The journey of deep insight is an intensely personal one, so we'll recommend ways to travel but we can't say what the destination will be for you.

At this point you're probably wondering why you should bother with the power of deep insight at all if it's so remote and inaccessible. In fact, it's exactly the opposite: The power of deep insight shows you how to be here, how to live with what you and others are, and how to bring about changes that will have long-lasting and beneficial consequences. This type of power is worth looking at because it shows you a way to understand, even improve, what's concretely in front of you, rather than using so much power to create (and hide out in) a fantasy world of "what ifs." We realize, however, that sometimes it's much less painful to retreat to the fantasy than it is to explore the dangers of your inner self.

With that caveat in mind, let's look at the use of deep insight in the power type we call the Sage.

THE POWER OF THE SAGE

The power of Sages stems from their deep insight into nothing less than the true nature of the universe. They can see that absolutely everything is connected, although to a Sage this doesn't mean endless chains of causation that need to be unraveled. It simply means that things (matter and energy) exist and by their very existence interact with other things. This isn't necessarily as lofty and inaccessible as it sounds. For example, remember that we said that Jackie was interested in discovering connections. One of the connections that is important to him is the physical-spiritual connection, and he works hard to understand how his beliefs interact with his wellness (or illness)—an interaction that the Shaman, whom we saw in the previous chapter, understands very well.

What Sages such as Jackie have discovered through their power of deep insight is that our minds create meaning out of interactions, and the meaning we create causes our happiness or suffering, makes us see ourselves as powerless or capable of improving our condition. Moreover, Sages know we have the power to make progress by changing our minds; that is, changing the meanings that we've made. In short, Sages would agree with one of their own, Shunryu Suzuki (who introduced Zen Buddhism to America), who believed that nothing good or bad ever happens outside our minds.

Now, that's a little far-fetched (you're thinking). Under what circumstances would your mind ever decide to give a positive (good) meaning to genocide or rape, for example? Well, your mind (as well as ours) probably can't answer that question, although a real Sage might have some enlightened words for all of us on the subject. Nevertheless, even if we leave out such knotty questions (which a Sage would not do), there is still plenty of room for deeply examining the meaning that we attach to more mundane items, and for seeing how that meaning affects us.

How can you do that? We'll give you more suggestions later on in the chapter, but here's the first: Whenever you are caught up in a negative situation or seem to be without options, the Sage within you can help you to think differently about the situation and how you're letting it affect you.

For example, the next time you feel like saying to your coworker, "You make me really mad when you talk so loudly on your personal phone calls," stop and look for the interconnections before you say anything. First of all, your coworker can't make you mad; you've made yourself mad. Why? Is it just because she talks loud, or is it because she's talking to her mother instead of working? Are you saying to yourself, "How dare she call her mother at work. She obviously has time for that but not for all the work she complains about!"

Can you change the meaning (from "I'm mad" to "I'd like to understand the problems with her workload" or "I'd like to find a way to tell her that her loudness is distracting to me") so that something productive can come from the situation? In other words, can you stop and look for deeper, systemic causes and solutions? After all, the loud voice and the fact that she's talking to her mother are two different issues. A lasting solution will depend on your ability to identify which one is really bothering you, and why.

In short, this fundamental aspect of Sage power, of looking deeply to understand connections and meanings, has a very real benefit for you in your everyday life that can be summed up this way:

It isn't necessary to feel or think about something in a predetermined way. Deliberately changing how you think and feel opens up options you didn't have before.

Sages can take a long look with the inner eye. This enables them to have deep insights about the raw materials of the universe (matter and energy), the meaning they make of them, and the effects of that meaning on people's behavior. This allows Sages to do the "right" thing at very fundamental levels. Let's see what underlies Sages' power that allows them to take that long look.

KEYS TO THE SAGE'S POWER

The ability to take a deep and sustained look into yourself or others or the universe requires the following, all of which characterize a Sage (we'll use Mohandes Gandhi, Martin Luther King, the Dalai Lama, and Mother Teresa as examples):

1. *An end to grasping and acquisitiveness.*
   Sages can gain an understanding of everything because they have let go of trying to have everything. In other words, Sages know that the way to understand something is to let it be, not bring it under your control. Since Sages have let go of grasping, they have little to lose. Their power is almost completely free of any thought that "I must have this or else"; that is, they have let go of personal ambition without becoming burned out. King and Gandhi, for example, knew that "equality" wasn't a thing they could own but a journey that could benefit everyone. They didn't try to grasp equality for themselves, they just tried to get (millions of) others to see it as a road worth taking.

2. *A belief that reality is constructed by us and therefore can be changed by us.*
   This begs the question of ultimate realities and ultimate beings, which we aren't going to address (but which a real Sage, again, probably could help us understand). Still, as we mentioned earlier, even leaving aside such thorny metaphysical issues, there are plenty of "realities" that you construct for yourself every day that either enhance or drain your power. For example, let's say you're not getting much attention from your boss. In one reality you say, "I did something wrong with that report. She's giving me the cold shoulder." In another reality you say, "She knows I've got that report to do, and she's leaving me alone so I can get it done." Both scenarios have exactly the same set of circumstances (matter and energy), but the reality (meaning) you've constructed around them, and its subse-

quent effect on you, is quite different. In short, Sages know that their power of deep insight can be blocked if they're distracted, annoyed, angry, worried, etc., about some aspect of their reality—so they work to change their perspective (which then changes the reality).

3. *The composure to not fight (but not cling to, either) the great fear that often comes with looking deeply inside.*
   This may be the most difficult key to the Sage's power. Those of you who have sat in meditation or used other deep-insight practices know that, sooner or later, some frightening or unpleasant insights are bound to come up. In fact, your psyche will go to great lengths to protect you by distracting your inner eye, inviting it to look at more pleasant fantasies. Sages can look at the ugly and scary parts of themselves, knowing that these too shall pass if they just let them go and don't interact. They understand that even pushing something away is an interaction. For example, in seeing the path that they were to follow, Gandhi and King may also have seen that it could very well lead to their deaths. (You can't take on such entrenched social meanings as race and class without making enemies of the people who have profited from those meanings.) Yet Gandhi and King let go of or made peace with the specter of a violent death, and although that death stopped them, the fear of it did not.

   Given these underpinnings of the Sage's power and the examples that we've just described, how might you see a Sage behaving in real life?

EIGHT CHARACTERISTICS OF THE SAGE

The power of deep insight leads a Sage to act in the following ways. Some of these may seem extreme; however, they are consistent with the Sage's belief that much more is possible than we usually imagine. Sages:

1. *Draw connections in the most unlikely (and enlightening) ways.*
   Because they've thought deeply about matter, energy, and mean-

ing, Sages can see interrelationships where others would miss them.

Example: Martin Luther King and Mohandes Gandhi saw, where others did not, the connection between nonviolent visibility and power. The prevailing wisdom (meaning) was that masses of people couldn't get what they wanted without resorting to violence—and we'd just had two world wars to prove it. Yet both men saw that it wasn't going to be enough for them to be making speeches, or for a few influential politicians to espouse racial equality; thousands needed to take to the streets (in, for example, what became the civil rights marches) to make this connection for the rest of us: that a mass of previously disenfranchised people now had power they were going to use not as a weapon for themselves but as a way to gain equality for everyone.

2. *Spend their power on the present.*
Sages know that relationships and connections only happen now and therefore can be changed now. They often take on global problems that seem unsolvable, then make progress with startling effectiveness because they see what can be done now. In other words, Sages seize an obvious problem in the here and now rather than spend all their time imagining what they might do in the future.

Example: King and his followers took to the streets (and buses) in local marches and demonstrations to promote local activities (such as voter registration) that had national impact.

3. *Share their vision in an understandable way.*
Even though Sages live in the present, they have a vision of the journey they're on and often have a compelling way of explaining it to others. Notice, though, that in keeping with Sages' nongrasping ways, they're more likely to cast their vision in terms of where you'll be rather than what you'll have at the end.

Example: King told his followers that on their shared journey toward equality, he had "been to the mountain top and seen the promised land," an inspiring and accessible vision if there ever was one.

4. *Are happy.*

   "The most important thing in life is to be happy," says Thich Nhat Hanh, a Vietnamese Buddhist monk (and Sage). Sages are happy (in a quiet sort of way) for all of the reasons we've stated in this chapter: They don't look for happiness in objects, and since they know they can change meaning and reality, they have many opportunities to see goodness and progress even in the gloomiest situations.

   Example: The Dalai Lama smiles and laughs quite a bit. Mother Teresa says she's happy with the work she does. Obviously, they're finding something that gives them joy in their difficult situations. Perhaps it's just knowing and deeply accepting that this is their work, that there is nowhere else to go, and that almost anything they do makes a difference.

5. *Guide others in their own self-exploration.*

   Sages can make it less frightening to plumb the depths yourself, for two reasons: They've already gone ahead and survived, and they've cast the journey in terms that you can understand.

   Example: The Dalai Lama has written extensively on how to explore your own consciousness and what you might find there. (We've listed some of his writings in the references section at the back of the book.) Martin Luther King went ahead to the "mountain top," which may have given others the courage they lacked to go there themselves.

6. *Believe they can improve the lot of all beings.*

   That's a tall order. How can you make a difference to every living thing? Sages know they can because of those interconnections that they so well understand. And they're willing to try because they know that influence often extends far beyond its intended target. This gives Sages the ability to bring about change where you might not expect it.

Example: The Dalai Lama's efforts to get the Chinese out of Tibet may have a very real and beneficial effect on that country's rapidly dwindling forests. Gandhi's philosophy of nonviolence has been used in countless civil power movements (including the one led by King) that the Indian never knew about.

7. *Treasure contemplation and nongrasping observation.*
An integral part of a Sage's life is time to meditate or reflect, not necessarily "on" anything but simply to rest the mind and allow matter, energy, and meaning to make themselves apparent.
Example: Gandhi urged his followers to meditate several times a day in order to quiet their busy minds and clear their inner vision.

8. *Are human.*
Although the description we've presented may make Sages sound like remote spiritual masters with superhuman powers, that is actually the opposite of the true characterization of a Sage. Sages are quintessentially human, perhaps more so than those who spend their time in a dream world of "what-if" and "If I'd only . . ." fantasies. Sages are right here, right now, being just what they are.
Example: None of the Sages we've used as examples are that much different from the rest of us. They make mistakes (sometimes fatal ones), and they have moral and ethical lapses (such as King's sexual indiscretions). They may sew their own clothes (Gandhi enjoyed spinning and weaving). Most importantly, they're out here with the rest of us, perhaps showing all of us how to participate more fully in the human life we have.

THE SAGE IN THE WORKPLACE

A Sage in an organization? Given what we've said so far, this sounds improbable. Even if such beings did exist, who would they be and what would they contribute?

In fact, Sages do exist in everyday organizations. You just seldom hear about them, and you may know none of them. Here are two clues to finding the Sages around you:

- They are the people who seem to always understand how the organization works, how to get things done, what will work, and whom to talk to (because they see the relationships and interconnections). They never use this knowledge manipulatively, but they're great at being able to get work done with even the most impossible boss, employee, or customer (because they believe they can improve everyone's lot).
- They are seldom senior managers, but no matter who they are, smart managers from top to bottom know about them and talk with them before making major decisions (because they encourage contemplation before action, and because they help others think deeply about themselves and the situation).

Unlike the other seven types, Sages will be useful to you in your organization even if they don't say or do anything overt. If you pay attention, a Sage's approach to life will highlight the overengineered (i.e., unnatural and unnecessary) aspects of your life and your organization, and will give you a plethora of examples of how to do more with less. One caution, though, if you manage or work with a Sage: They are hard to rouse to action. Sages just don't see a crisis or fire drill around every corner. In addition, they realize that sometimes the best course of action is to do nothing. When Sages perceive that people and the organization are being seriously harmed by misguided ego and ambition, though, they act.

THE SAGE'S RELATIONSHIP
WITH OTHER TYPES

We've already mentioned in previous chapters that the positive power types can all benefit from a relationship with a Sage, who will help them see even more deeply into their own power. (Sages would say that they themselves benefit from relations with all power types, since each one shows them new interconnections.)

On the other hand, Sages aren't going to be defeated by the less effective power types. Those types will relentlessly try to remove Sages from their "territory," since Sages can see through every last one of their games and smoke screens. In the end, Sages know that defeat (like empowerment) is a state of mind that can't be "done" to another person. Even death doesn't usually extinguish the power of a Sage.

PROBLEMS OF THE SAGE

For all their wisdom and deep understanding, Sages (being human) may run into a couple of major problems:

1. They can be very intimidating. Sages can see right through your defenses, even those you didn't know you had. In addition, they can see what's really going on at deep levels where you may prefer not to look. If you know a Sage and are worried about his or her "power," realize that Sages aren't trying to "catch" you and that their insights may help you learn more about yourself.

2. They often get banished, and sometimes get killed. Since Sages see things that others wish would remain hidden and take on causes that often disrupt the status quo, they're not likely to be popular with those in (corrupt) power. King and Gandhi were assassinated; the Dalai Lama runs a religion and government in exile. While it isn't likely that Sages in your organization will have this problem, you should be aware that Sages make good layoff targets, especially if they've been vocal about poor management practices or working conditions.

Although the power of deep insight we've just described seems universally beneficial, there is a way to employ it for manipulative and self-serving ends. It's used this way by people who seem very Sage-like (at least to their followers), but who somewhere along the line forgot that the journey was for everyone. Unlike true Sages, these people don't tolerate any connections, realities, or thoughts (especially spiritual ones) that they haven't defined or sanctioned. Their ambition is to achieve immortality by creating a perfect future world in which they will be idolized (perhaps as a god) for having brought it about. The followers of this type happily and wholeheartedly (if not thoughtfully) bow to their leader's power and embrace and implement any ideas and directions that come from that source.

We don't think you'll run into too many of this type in a typical workplace, so we won't deal any further with them here. They tend to create mega-organizations (nations, usually), and then give them the rules to live by and the slogans to use in place of thought—a total and all-encompassing use of power that's tough to pull off in regular-size workplaces.

We've summarized the essential characteristics of the Sage in the box here.

Essential Characteristics of the Sage

Sages . . .
- understand interconnections
- focus on improving the present
- share their vision with you
- model happiness
- help others to plumb the depth and breadth of the self
- vow to save all beings
- encourage contemplation
- embrace their humanness

MOVING TOWARD THE POWER OF THE SAGE

How do you get to be a Sage? Unfortunately, we don't think there's a direct route. Sages are what all of the other personal power types become when they've fully realized (and let go of) those roles. However, there are practices that Sages use to understand and enhance their power that can help all of us develop our personal power, whatever its type. (And if you're concerned that you may be one of the less effective types, the practices of the Sage can help you lessen that power, and increase the more effective power that's within you.)

Our suggestions for moving toward the power of the Sage within you are listed below. We also recommend that you find a Sage with whom you can spend some time. Sage power is next to impossible to attain by yourself, and it is transferable to some extent. Just spending time with a Sage without doing anything overt will increase your own power of deep insight.

PRACTICING THE POWER OF DEEP INSIGHT

The following methods of bringing about deep understanding may not automatically give you the power of the Sage, but they will move you along in your own personal power, whatever type that may be.

- Notice how you're feeling and what you're thinking, without trying to hold onto or find the cause of either. Notice that you're angry, for example, but don't immediately leap to the connection "because they didn't get the report to me on time." Maybe something about the report is connected to your anger (perhaps it unpleasantly reminds you of what happened the last time you delivered a report late). Or maybe the anger and the report just came up at the same time and actually have nothing to do with each other.

This may seem like an odd way to gain a deep understanding of connections; however, such an understanding requires that you first let go of the (often spurious) connections that you're accustomed to making, especially between actions and feelings and especially when you find yourself saying, "It/ you made me feel. . . ."

- Change the meaning of events, and notice how their effect on you changes. Once you've disconnected your thoughts and feelings from external events, take an event that used to "make" you feel one way and deliberately try to feel differently about it. You'll soon see that, in many cases, you have a choice about your reaction to a situation, and that choice gives you more options for improving the situation. You may not be able to make yourself happy in all cases, but you may be able to see some alternatives (i.e., some ways to not be stuck and angry) that you previously didn't have. For example, try choosing to be relieved and elated that the report was late. The delay gave you time to attend to some pressing issues that would have distracted you from the report, anyway. Now when the report arrives, you can give it your undivided attention.

  Consciously changing your reality is one of the best ways to counteract any of the seven alter egos within you. The Controller, for example, can choose to be relieved (instead of panicked) when all of the details aren't piled up on her desk. The Gamester can think differently about his reaction when other people win.

- When deep understandings do arise, and they're unpleasant or frightening, reach out to someone (even if that person isn't a Sage). Unfortunately, the first suggestion we made about just noticing (rather than reacting to) how you're feeling and what you're thinking doesn't work very well when truly scary things come up. These might include thoughts of death, feelings of abandonment, or concerns about being unloved.

It's difficult to just notice those things without immediately getting sucked into a power-draining fantasy or physical reaction. For example, you've discovered that your anger about the late report actually connected to feelings of rage that you felt when a long-time partner refused to acknowledge your existence.

To protect you from these painful feelings, a fantasy might immediately arise in which you get even with the partner, or get noticed by some famous person and therefore don't need your partner's attention.

- We've found that writing letters (even if they never get mailed) is a good way to work through some of those deeply unpleasant understandings. A letter gives you the chance to mull over and refine your understanding, under the safe and comforting guise of explaining it to someone else.

Above all, learning to find and trust the power of your deep insights takes time and a quiet place. Give yourself a gift of both. (We believe that the only way to enhance Sage power in the world is to encourage environments of contemplation and seeking-without-grasping.) It also helps if you can find someone who's further along the path to guide you.

SUMMING IT UP: THE POWER OF THE SAGE

We end our descriptions of the types of personal power with the power of the Sage. This is a power of deep understanding: of seeing connections, of creating realities, and of realizing options that will improve our lives and the lives of others. It's a power that doesn't come easily, yet one that can be of help even if you aren't a Sage yourself.

We'll borrow the Dalai Lama's words to recap the importance of this power for all of us:

> *In today's highly interdependent world, individuals and nations can no longer resolve many of their problems by themselves. We need one another. We must therefore develop a sense of universal responsibility. It is our collective and individual responsibility to protect and nurture the global family, to support its weaker members, and to preserve and tend to the environment in which we all live.* (A Policy of Kindness, pp. 113-14.)

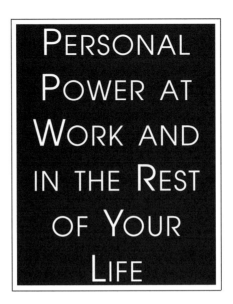

PERSONAL POWER AT WORK AND IN THE REST OF YOUR LIFE

U p to now, this book has been about how you can find and develop your own career power within yourself, rather than expecting it to come from your boss or your company or organization. Why have we focused so much on the workplace?

The United States, like many other countries, is caught in a potentially devastating cycle: Since the 1980s, the rich are getting richer while the poor get poorer. Economists now suggest that this division is beginning to drag down worker productivity on a broad basis. Yet they're also suggesting that the problem has less to do with the traditional scapegoat, technology (which actually creates more jobs than it eliminates), and more to do with who has the power and how they use it in the workplace. (Education also plays a major part. We didn't focus on that directly in this book, although you probably gleaned that the personally powerful types are much more open to learning than are their alter egos.)

Since you will spend perhaps one-third of your life in a workplace setting, it's important to your personal sense of "richness" or "poorness" (in both economic and other terms) that you understand the following choice: You can allow powerful forces to determine how you make your living and how you react when that living gets taken away (during downsizing and layoffs), or you can identify and develop your power within to make yourself employable in a world where job security is a thing of the past. As we've shown in the preceding chapters, the ability to be portable and flexible and to feel competent and secure in terms of how and where you apply your talents will help to ensure that you get to have a "career."

PORTABLE JOB POWER = PORTABLE LIFE POWER

Once you've found your power within, you'll discover that it has applicability beyond the workplace. In this chapter, we'll take that next step and describe how to extend your power to other aspects of your life. In particular, we're going to emphasize how you can deal powerfully with intimidating institutions that seem bent on taking your power away. We'll point out that a major factor in the apparent power of these institutions is that you voluntarily (and very prematurely) surrender your own power to them when you walk through their doors. In short, this chapter suggests that:

> *Personal power is something that you carry with you from place to place; it doesn't need to wait outside while you go in.*

In addition to translating your personal job power to your dealings with institutions, we'll take a look at personal power in four other settings: in your relationships, in how you live in a materialistic culture, in how you contribute to the world, and in how you develop your spiritual base. We'll also describe some roadblocks you may encounter in your job and elsewhere as you exercise your personal power, and we'll end with some suggestions for developing and using your power regardless of the setting.

First, though, let's review the types of power we presented in this book, and translate their major characteristics into broad principles that will help you to extend your power beyond the workplace.

RECAPPING THE PERSONAL POWER TYPES

You will find the personal power types and their alter egos in your workplace and in almost all other aspects of your life. Those types of power and the primary ways they are used (and abused) can be summarized as follows:

1. The power of *sustained strategic thinking*, which Kings and Queens use to see the long-term context and its implications (and which Controllers use in an effort to direct every detail of how the future comes to be).

2. The power to *win with glory and honor*, which Warriors use to bring lasting success to themselves, their colleagues, and their organizations (and which Gamesters use to keep from losing the attention of those in power).

3. The power to *lend your power to others* in support of their efforts, which Aides do without losing their own identity (and which Co-Dependents do in order to meet their own unacknowledged needs for worth and belonging).

4. The power to *use what's at hand to change the situation*, through which Builders make everyone more productive (and through

which Rebels prove that they are different, whether the difference is productive or not).

5. The power to *change the problem or situation by perceiving it differently*, which Artists use to find new solutions or possibilities (and which Loners use to protect their own solitude by creating problems for others to solve).

6. The power to *discern what's effective and ineffective*, which stems from the Judge's consistent moral base (and from Preachers' desire to prove that their moral base is right and yours is wrong).

7. The power to *identify and treat illness*, which the Shaman uses to restore emotional and spiritual (as well as physical) health (and which the Shrink uses to keep you "sick" by imposing standards— treatments—that you can never quite live up to).

8. The power to *see connections and new meanings through deep insight*, which the Sage uses to get unstuck from life-robbing ways of thinking and acting.

In addition, all the positive power types have discovered the underlying key to personal power: The more you use, the more you have. This principle will help you to feel that you have enough personal power in all aspects of your life. You don't need to store it or ration it, for this basic reason: The more you release your personal power, the more you will inspire and give confidence to others in the effective use of their own power (which ultimately cuts down on your workload).

On the other hand, the alter egos hoard power (and try to tap yours), apparently in the mistaken belief that there's a limited supply. Although the alter egos seem powerful, they're generally ineffective in sustaining their power over the long haul, primarily because they're doing so much of the work themselves.

PERSONAL POWER AT WORK

Before taking a look at how you can translate your personal job power to the rest of your life, let's recap why exercising your power is especially important in the workplace.

It's quite possible that in other aspects of your life you may act and feel more powerful than you do at work. Unfortunately, you and others (especially the alter egos) may believe or hope that your power stays in the parking lot. We think this is a dangerous belief, especially in the economic environment we described earlier in this chapter. Using your power in the way you earn a living means several things other than the (traditional) definition of defining and controlling your own work. Remember that for the eight personal power types, job power does not necessarily mean having power or control over others or over all aspects of their work. (In the case of Aides, for example, it means loaning their power to others.)

Exercising your personal power at work does mean that:

1. You are engaged in work in which you find fulfillment and creative release in whatever you're doing (from designing buildings to typing letters). Said differently, it means that you aren't fighting or rebelling against the activity that produces your paycheck.

2. If you are not engaged in work that is creative or fulfilling (due to some circumstance that truly is beyond your control), you nevertheless acknowledge that the work does provide you with basic necessities. This is an important point: Not all personally powerful people are in jobs they love; however, in such situations they aren't trying to make the work do something for them that it cannot (bring them fulfillment, happiness, etc.). If circumstances make you earn a living that is without crea-

tive expression, then using your power in that setting means that:

- you recognize exactly what the work does provide (even if it's only money)
- you aren't trying to get anything else out of the job
- you develop other settings for fulfilling your creative needs
  If you're fighting what you're doing for a living, then you're not acting powerfully; in fact, your power is being drained away by the struggle.

3. You release power in your colleagues not by telling them what to do but by using your own power to modify the organization. Then the organization, instead of trying to "give" (or take) power, stays out of workers' way so that they can effectively do their jobs (i.e., discover and develop their own power). Note that this doesn't necessarily mean that you add layers or procedures to the organization; rather, it may mean that you remove key restraints that have always kept workers "in line."

4. You want to go to work, and you want to go home. Even powerful people who love their jobs know that it can't meet all of their needs. (If it did, it might actually mean that their nonwork relationships were out of whack and that they were staying at work to avoid them.) If either home or work is an escape from the other, then you are powerful in neither.

5. You are portable. That is, you are passionate and committed to the task, but you could walk away from the particular workplace tomorrow. You may be wondering, "How can I possibly act powerfully when I might get laid off?" Being portable means using your power regardless of whether your current job will last (it won't) or whether the next job will be there (it will). It means that you have confidence in your skill set, in your ability to learn, and in your

ability to manage your reaction to situations (including layoffs) that is independent of any particular workplace. In other words, even if you love the job you have now, you could (through your own choice or a "downsizing") make your living elsewhere. This confidence in your own competence is the essence of portable job power.

When you begin to find your own personal power at work, you'll also quickly discover that you can't confine it there. Let's now look at how the principles and types of personal power translate to the nonwork aspects of your life.

Personal Power for the Rest of Your Life

We deliberately chose the words "rest of your life" for the title of this chapter and section because it conveys at least three meanings, all of which are important to the exercise of your personal power.

First, there is the meaning to which we just alluded: The rest of your life is the nonwork part that we haven't yet discussed in this book. Second, the rest of your life also means "the years you have to live." We believe that developing your own personal power will help you be effective during most or all of that time (especially when the workplace is no longer where you exercise most or any of your power). Finally, "rest" also means the ability to pause from exertion. Using your personal power wisely allows you to stop and recharge your power, which means that you'll have more energy because you won't be draining it away on power-wasting activities. And you'll need that extra energy not only at work but in the nonwork areas we describe below.

As we mentioned earlier, personal power is something that you carry with you from place to place; it doesn't need to stay outside while you go in, even if you're going into the most intimidating organization or institution. In fact, you'll find that acting powerfully in any setting increases your overall power. Let's see how you might translate your personal power at work to five nonwork situations. In each case, we'll describe an effective type of personal power that you can use, as well as how an alter ego might make the situation worse.

DEALING POWERFULLY WITH ESTABLISHED INSTITUTIONS

Large, bureaucratic organizations (of government, medicine, and education, in particular) can pose a severe threat to your sense of personal power. Because of the laws and regulations that govern them, the amount of certification required to join them, and the significant (even life-threatening) events and decisions that routinely happen in them, these institutions can seem like one big Controller. This may have the effect of turning you into a Co-Dependent when you're dealing with them; you'll do anything to please them so they'll get off your case.

How to use your power: Dealing with powerful institutions means only one thing: Remembering and acting on the fact that you are the customer of those institutions. Regardless of how controlling and intimidating these places might be, and regardless of how much they profess to know what's good for you, the bottom line is that you are paying for their services, which by itself gives you plenty of power.

On the other hand, don't confuse the controlling nature of the organization with the individual people who are trying to help you. In recent years, the ideas and practices of customer service have permeated even the most bureaucratic of these organizations, and we've found many Warriors and Aides, in particular, in these places who will give you their support and work for your cause.

Here are our suggestions for dealing powerfully with established institutions. First, make a list of exactly what you want or what questions you have before you go. When you arrive at the institution and begin talking with the staff, the most important step is to get whomever you're dealing with to move at your speed. These places often work with specialized vocabulary (including plenty of acronyms) and complex procedures. If you don't understand, ask. And keep asking until you're comfortable.

In addition, don't assume that the path they suggest is the only one or the best one. Ask about alternatives. If you're not getting the service you want, say so (calmly) to the person you're dealing with, thank them for their efforts, and ask to see a supervisor. When the course of action has been selected, ask exactly what will happen and what the institution needs from you, reiterate what you need from the staff, and (most importantly) ask about common errors or omissions that might slow up the process. In short, stand your ground until your needs are met or until an alternative is agreed upon by all, and if you're feeling rushed or railroaded, say so.

Positive power example: Ray (a Warrior) has received two notices from the Internal Revenue Service about an audit. He returned both notices promptly, although the second notice said that no response had been received. The second notice seemed very threatening, mentioning legal action and a compounding of interest if the taxes in question weren't paid. Ray is concerned, but he isn't intimidated.

He calls the local IRS office and asks for an exact explanation of the audit procedure, which he gets (after asking several questions about deadlines, forms, and situations that usually flag a tax return for an audit). After the explanation, the agent tells Ray that her computer shows that neither of his two notices have been returned. Ray doesn't argue with the agent; instead, he asks her to note in the comment field on his computer record the dates on which he returned the notices. The agent then suggests that Ray bring his tax records to her IRS office (120 miles away) and resolve the situation in person. Ray thanks her for the suggestion but says that he's unwilling to drive that far. Could she send his file to a closer office? The agent can't authorize that, so Ray asks to speak with her supervisor.

The supervisor gives Ray the address of a nearby office. Ray asks the supervisor to call the agent who will handle Ray's case in the local office and explain the situation, so that Ray doesn't have to start from scratch with a new agent. When Ray arrives at the local office with his documents, the new agent is ready and they are able to close the audit within an hour.

Alter ego example: Adele (a Rebel) has been at the local community hospital for the past two days with her mother, who was admitted with blurred vision and a high fever. Several times staff members have explained to Adele the procedures and monitoring equipment that test for various illnesses, but Adele will have none of it. No one is going to treat her mother like every other sick person who wanders in off the street.

In addition, Adele feels that the rules about visitors are ridiculous, so she has secretly stayed in her mother's room on both nights to keep an eye on the monitoring equipment herself and make sure that nothing goes wrong. She's alternately up and pestering or arguing with the staff or slumped in the waiting room chair feeling like no one is paying attention. The whole hospital, with all of its rules and regulations, makes her so mad. Why can't they just get to the diagnosis and treatment, so she and her mother can get out of there?

The stories of Ray and Adele illustrate an important point about using your power with bureaucratic institutions: Trying to change their myriad regulations and procedures will only drain your power; however, that doesn't mean that you just give up and play by their rules. Instead, use your power to understand the rules and hierarchies of the system so that you can use them to your advantage. This requirement to work powerfully within the system makes the Warrior an effective type of power to use when dealing with bureaucratic institutions.

ACTING POWERFULLY IN YOUR RELATIONSHIPS

Your personal relationships, both close and casual, may represent a difficult venue for the use of your power, especially if one partner has strong alter ego tendencies (especially of the Controller or Co-Dependent variety). However, being in a relationship doesn't require you or others to give up power. On the contrary, using your power to form relationships in which both (or all) parties can be open, honest, caring, and concerned, and still feel free, boosts the power level of all involved.

How to use your power: A key to using your power in a relationship involves paying close attention to when someone's power (yours or your partner's) is being drained. This usually happens because of some mistaken or unclarified idea about what the other person wants or about what will make them happy. This can quickly deteriorate into "you make me feel . . ." discussions where blame and guilt are followed by the silent treatment.

We think that the best way to prevent or resolve such situations in relationships is to use your power to communicate. Never, never expect the other person to be a mind reader (nor try to be one yourself). Help yourself and your partner to clarify what you both want. State what you're feeling (especially if you're frightened or angry, when you tend to withdraw), and say what you're picking up from the other person even if they're being quiet (but don't "accuse" them of not talking to you). Ask if their needs are being met, and state how yours are and are not being fulfilled. Most of all, be clear within yourself whenever you think you're doing something "for" your partner. Are you sure you aren't doing it just for you? How will you feel if your partner doesn't notice what you've done? One of the greatest drains on your power in a relationship is feeling resentful when your efforts aren't appreciated, and the best use of your power is to ask, listen, and check back.

Positive power example: Muriel (a Shaman) is in a relationship where her partner is going through some tough times at work and with his aging parents. Since he's distracted with these problems, he's lost sleep, tends to cry easily, and has wondered aloud about why bad things happen to good people. Muriel, who's been paying attention to his emotional and spiritual symptoms, as well as the physical ones, has developed some strategies that seem to be working for both her and her partner. First, she realizes that just being with him, even in silence, makes him feel less lonely. Second, Muriel has discovered that initiating a conversation about her own fears causes her partner to open up about what's bothering him. Finally, she realizes that there is quite a bit of "sickness" in her partner's life right now; therefore, she sees to it that the two of them spend some time each week with a few close friends who are healthy and who can provide a reminder to her partner that life isn't always out of balance.

Alter ego example: Ron (Muriel's older brother and a Co-Dependent) is watching his sister go through this tough time with her partner. Ron resigned himself to Muriel's living arrangements long ago, but he is now determined that Muriel isn't going to be dragged down by her partner's problems. Ron calls Muriel every day at work with advice about what her partner should do. Ron has even researched retirement homes and sent brochures to Muriel's partner in the hope that he'll get his parents into a home so that Muriel won't be stuck taking care of them. Ron paid for a weekend spa treatment for Muriel so that she could "get away from it all" (and was then miffed when Muriel changed the reservation so that her partner could go with her). Ron knows that all his life he has taken care of his kid sister, and with his help she'll get through this crisis too.

As you saw with Muriel, getting thoughts, feelings, and fears out into the open, and being able to support the other person without losing yourself (which Ron did not do), are keys to using your power effectively in your relationships. The power of the Shaman or the Aide will help you here (although you need to be careful about your Aide, in particular, slipping into Controller or Co-Dependent behaviors if your own needs aren't being met). If the relationship is already in trouble, you should monitor the tendency in yourself or the other person to become a Shrink, believing that it's the other person who has the problem, needs to go to therapy, etc.

DEALING POWERFULLY WITH THE CULTURE OF ACQUISITION

From morning to night, our culture wants to addict you to things (i.e., to make you dependent and coming back for more). You can't truly have fun, so the messages say, unless you have an exotic vacation, the right beer, a womanly or manly scent, and myriad other accoutrements guaranteed to make you a better person. You'll find, however, that this relentless acquisition drains your power rather than giving you more of it. You must put considerable effort into finding and buying things and enjoying them (i.e., showing them off) once you have them. The catch is that having things doesn't make you feel as powerful as you expected—so you go for more.

How to use your power: The key to using your power in such a culture is to learn to appreciate things without becoming attached to them (i.e., without having to own them in one way or another). We have no illusions about what we're asking you to do here: Tuning out the messages from the culture of acquisition is very difficult; however, you probably already sense that that culture is draining your power.

So here are our suggestions for dissuading yourself from a belief that you must have it all. The first step is to examine your motivations, especially if you are tempted with a large "purchase" (involving money, time, emotional commitment, or some other valuable resource). The second step, assuming that the purchase is still important to you, is to see if you can get the same result in a less costly way. Try asking yourself these four questions before you buy:

- Why do I think I need to have this?
- What do I expect it to do for me?

- Can I get the need met another way?
- Is this a situation in which I can just wait it out until the need goes away?

The strategies we've mentioned so far are still about getting a tangible result for yourself. The next step is to slow down and appreciate what you already have, to take stock of all of your needs that are already being met (to "stop and smell the roses," as the saying goes). We know that this is even harder than the steps we suggested above. However, once again you'll use less power if you appreciate how much is already being done that you don't need to duplicate or reinvent or acquire.

Positive power example: Gayle (an Artist) is writing a book for new managers. The publisher has given her a large advance, which Gayle has no plans to spend. There isn't anything in particular that she's been wanting to have. What she really wants is to open the eyes of new managers to all the positive and self-fulfilling aspects of guiding other people to achieve and appreciate a job well done. Gayle herself used to believe in (and covet) a management reward system based on money and perks. She worked in such a system for years.

However, what she discovered is that she feels most productive and most worthwhile as a human being when she's writing, and again when her readers tell her that what she wrote made a difference in their lives. It's this feeling, more than anything else, that Gayle wants to have, and she can get it by writing from experiences that she's already had.

Alter ego example: Tony (a Gamester) lives by a bit of bumper-sticker philosophy, "Whoever has the most toys wins." The toy, in Tony's case, is software. He has the latest version of hundreds of programs and prides himself on being able to use them all. Moreover, he spends nights and weekends scouring trade magazines for tips and gossip about the program's creators and how the program was put together.

Tony likes to have that "inside knowledge" because it makes him a favorite of some owners of big computer stores who always consult with him on what to put on their shelves. (If someone does happen to display more knowledge of a program than Tony does, he quickly dismisses the program as "not worth it" or says "you're making a mistake using that one.")

The key to using your power in the culture of acquisition is to not let yourself be worn out by the pursuit of ownership and the (perhaps guilty) need to use and enjoy something once you have it. You get the sense that Gayle and Tony are both using considerable power to have something; however, Gayle is transforming what she already has (experience and insight about management) while Tony is wearing himself out with the ever-new.

The Artist (who trades in perceptions rather than things) and the Sage (who has pretty much given up things and can be with something without having to own it) are good power guides for dealing with the culture of acquisition.

MAKING A POWERFUL CONTRIBUTION TO THE WORLD

Making a contribution in a global setting has two meanings: that you use some of your power to improve the lot of other beings (children, endangered species, or redwoods, for example), and, conversely, that you avoid activities that drain the power of others. This sounds daunting: How are you supposed to fit charitable works into your already overloaded schedule? We respond: Perhaps that schedule already includes an activity that makes a difference; or perhaps you don't need to be doing all of the items on your schedule, which would give you time to make your contribution.

How to use your power: Sages believe they can save all beings, and they aren't defeated by the thought of changing the world one person at a time. However, you don't need to be a Sage to make a powerful contribution. The first step is to think carefully about what's

important to you in the world (a good exercise of your Judge power).
The second step is to do one or more of the following (in ascending
order of power use):

- Take something that you already do and make it into a contribution. (When you're shopping for groceries, pick up a few extra items and put them in the canned-food bin that the store
  maintains for a local charity.)
- Identify something extra that you can do that doesn't drain
  your power. (Making books-on-tape for the blind can be done
  at home on your own schedule.)
- Re-examine where you currently use your power, and change
  your life so that more of your power goes to others—in Aide-
  like fashion. (Get a job with fewer hours that's closer to home
  so that you can take the time you used to spend commuting
  and spend it volunteering at a local institution.)

Positive power example: Richard (a Builder) is a management
consultant. He has become increasingly concerned about organizations
that treat people with socially stigmatized diseases, such as AIDS.
These organizations often have difficulty retaining staff, managing
cash flow, and getting the message out about their services to those
who most need them—areas in which Richard has considerable experience.

Richard's consulting business keeps him very busy, but he offers
to make a presentation to the local hospice board one evening, and
gives them some suggestions about how they might take what they're
already doing and fine-tune it to manage their business more effectively. Later, he volunteers to create a couple of public service messages for the hospice.

Over time, Richard sees the desperate nature of the hospice's
clients and begins to scale back his consulting practice so that he
can give more time to a cause that is becoming increasingly
important to him. (He tells himself that while he may have to live

with less, some of these people aren't going to live at all without his help.)

Alter ego example: Vickie (a Loner) is disturbed by the many things that are going wrong on the planet: global warming, childhood malnutrition, destruction of wildlife areas. She'd like to help, but the problems seem overwhelming, and she's afraid that all of her energy and freedom would be sucked away if she were just another volunteer among hundreds of others during her time off from work. So Vickie has joined several conservation groups via mail. She figures that her dues must be doing some good. In addition, she's making a contribution by reading the groups' publications and informing herself about their issues.

Making a global contribution is all about sharing your power. Which again brings up this equation: The more of your personal power you use, the more you'll have. Vickie doesn't believe this, but Richard is beginning to see that he doesn't need all the power he has and that he can make a real difference by diverting some of his power to the powerless. The power of the Builder and the Aide within you will help you to make a contribution; the far-seeing power of the King or Queen might help you contribute on a larger scale than you thought possible.

PRACTICING A POWERFUL SPIRITUALITY

Does this mean becoming a church member? It might, although using your power to develop your spirituality may bear little relationship to organized religion and outward religiosity. Ideas like "love," "compassion," "the brotherhood and sisterhood of us all," and "a deeper meaning in life" aren't passé; they support you in rediscovering the spiritual base of human life and then living out of it.

How to use your power: Being spiritual isn't just for Sages or Shamans. It's for all of the personal power types within you. In addition, it implies a very personal journey, which is why we can't give you many concrete suggestions for practicing it. We do suggest the following, however:

- Regularly create quiet time for yourself in which you can examine your values and reflect on your behavior in light of those values.
- Consider the concrete world in front of you as just one of many valid sources of perception and information, and learn to listen to other sources around you (which you might call feelings, or intuition, or faith).

Positive power example: Ed (a Judge) closes his office door for 15 minutes each afternoon and spends the time in quiet reflection. What new insights about how to do his job better and how to treat his colleagues more effectively did he learn from the morning's work? Did he listen to others in a way that helped him understand their perspective? Is he applying his values to his actions and interactions? What about the tension he senses around the office: Is it really there, or is he bringing some of his own anxieties into the way he interprets others' actions?

Alter ego example: Julie (a Preacher) knows what's best for everyone. She prides herself on being able to see right through the defenses and beliefs that confine others to their small worlds. She's right about how things really are, and anyone who sees things differently needs to "get real." She belittles those "dreamers" who indulge in reflection and contemplation (and doing it herself makes her restless and anxious to be up and doing something).

The ability to practice spiritual power is the ability to ask questions and live with an answer you didn't expect (including no answer at all). Spiritual power reduces ambiguity by giving you access to more sources of information and by (ultimately) showing you what a Sage sees: the interconnection of all things. All of the positive power types can seek a deeper spiritual nature by simply going deeper into the type itself. All of the alter egos avoid that activity; it might show the holes in their carefully constructed defenses.

As you extend your personal power from your work to the rest of your life, you will find that the same principles and behaviors apply in a variety of settings. You will also find that the road isn't always smooth. So, before we close this chapter with some final thoughts on personal power, we'll take a look at obstacles that you may encounter in developing and exercising your power.

PERSONAL POWER PROBLEMS

Tapping your personal power isn't always easy. It requires unlearning a lifetime of negative messages and behaviors. Moreover, it runs counter to all but the most recent management theories, which have traditionally taken a controlling or parental approach. Personal power, despite its appeal, seems to ignore the fact that most of us work in organizations that have thrived for a long time on those older management theories. Too much effort would be required, perhaps, to have so many workers and managers unlearn lifelong patterns of behavior so that they and others can do work differently. Often, only start-ups and other entrepreneurial organizations see personal power as a necessity (instead of a luxury), because they simply can't afford to have nonpowerful people around.

In this section we'll take a look at four situations in which developing and using your own power may not have the beneficial consequences you assumed. These situations happen when:

1. *Organizational and individual needs diverge.*
   In those start-up organizations that we just mentioned, you and the organization probably are using the same kind of power in the same direction (since you all have the same goal—to get this great new idea off the ground). However, over time, your needs (for ful-

fillment of your power) and the organization's need (for sustainable profit) may diverge; that is, your objectives have less and less to do with organizational objectives. Older or less entrepreneurial organizations, even those that espouse "empowerment," eventually run into the problem that powerful individuals recognize when personal and organizational objectives diverge. And powerful individuals usually choose in favor of their personal goals and needs. This may leave the organization with an abundance of employees who haven't yet developed their personal power. It may leave you, as a user of personal power, without an organization in which you comfortably can belong and contribute. You may have trouble finding an organization in which you can exercise your personal power without feeling so constrained that your creativity is blocked.

2. *Finding and using your power creates its own angst.*
Exercising your power can actually generate rejection and fear in your acquaintances and coworkers. The power of creativity and freedom, and the need for self-disclosure and self-examination that comes with them, also carries the risk of embarrassment and threat for those who feel less powerful than you do. Some people just can't "put themselves out there" in the way that personally powerful people can. Worse, people who are acting powerfully may not be of much help; instead of being perceived as role models, they may only seem remote and intimidating to their less powerful colleagues.

3. *Powerful people (and their bosses or colleagues) seem to be hard to manage, hard to work for, or hard to work with.*
If you're using your personal power and finding fulfillment therein, it's likely that the traditional rewards and norms of behaviors that have kept many organizations alive no longer appeal to you. From your colleagues' perspective, you're "getting away" with behaviors that they wouldn't dream of, and you're not responding appropri-

ately to the perks that are handed out. Since a major difference between powerful and nonpowerful people is their horizon of possibilities, your less powerful colleagues will resent the license that you seem to take for granted (not realizing, of course, that your power to do "special" things and feel rewarded is available to them too).

4. *Your "spirit" of empowerment is genuinely strong, but the "flesh" of infrastructure is weak in terms of its ability to support your power.* Sometimes, despite your most powerful and creative efforts, the systems and policies of your organization just can't accommodate your visions. Imagine, for example, the clash between powerful behavior and the behavior for which most performance appraisal systems reward you. Or try to buy the computer system for your office that would most empower you and see what the MIS department has to say about your choice.

In some of these cases, you may need to find a different organization to belong to, or simply wait for a critical mass of powerful people to develop. To help you, we've created a final checklist of do's and don'ts for exercising your personal power on p. 230.

Do's and Don'ts of Personal Power

DO use your power in relationships with others.
DON'T try to be powerful in a vacuum.

DO see yourself as a contributor and a learner.
DON'T try to one-up others (nor put yourself always at the bottom).

DO give equal attention to the needs and feelings of others.
DON'T focus just on your own fulfillment.

DO listen.
DON'T force others to hear you.

DO change your mind or admit that you're wrong when appropriate.
DON'T try to convert others.

DO stay in the present and deal with the joys and obstacles there.
DON'T get lost in a fantasy-perfect world.

DO focus on what might be done.
DON'T look for scapegoats.

DO imagine alternatives and possibilities.
DON'T imagine threats and constraints that aren't there.

DO pause and reflect.
DON'T mask your fear with busywork.

DO accept some ambiguity.
DON'T force clarity before its time.

And finally, the most important action you can take is to ask for help:

DO find a role model or mentor to help you develop your power.
DON'T try to go it alone.

The Key: Finding a Mentor

To bring the power of each positive type alive within you, it will help to find a role model, even if he or she is a fictional one in a favorite book. Think about your mentor in light of the following questions:

- Which characteristics from each of the "Essential Differences" box in each chapter do you see most strongly in this person?
- How would you describe his or her specific behaviors as an exemplar of that particular power type?
- What is the impact of these behaviors on you? (How do they make you think and feel?)
- Do you see any specific behaviors in yourself that you'd like to enhance (regardless of which power type you are)? If so, you might observe the person you just identified. He or she can help you by showing you how to use your personal power.

Summing It Up: The Rewards of Personal Power

After all you've read in the preceding chapters on personal power, its up sides and down sides, the things to do and the things not to do, why should you embark on the journey that we've outlined in this book? Here are five reasons; perhaps by now you have thought of others:

1. You will have a better sense of control over your own destiny. The positive power types have shown you how much you can get done, and the alter egos have shown you specifically where you might derail your own efforts.

2. You will have a clearer sense of what's important (i.e., worth expending your resources on) and what's not. One of the major principles of all personal power is that it requires you to take a look within at what you want and need (probably less than you thought) and at what you are realistically capable of (probably more than you thought).

3. You will know who belongs in your organization and relationships and who doesn't. You'll be able to distinguish the effective power types from their less effective counterparts, and grow the former while revealing the disruptiveness of the latter. Moreover, you'll be able to tell whether or not YOU belong in certain workplaces and relationships. With a good sense of your own power, you'll see where your needs and talents match, and you won't be deceiving yourself or others if they diverge.

4. You will have more energy. As we already mentioned several times, using your personal power gives you more energy because you aren't trying to duplicate (one-up) someone else's effort and you aren't doing things that no one wants.

5. Finally, you will get real work done, instead of spending your energy on workarounds and fancy footwork to defend yourself.

Our premise throughout this book has been that there is no powerful organization or workplace, only individuals acting powerfully to meet business and personal goals. Our summary message here is that you can't make others powerful; however, you can release your own power, which will inspire others to activate their own power grid.

This means that all of the types of power happen in a relationship, and that positive power affirms the self, others, and the relationship itself. It also means that personal power is not a place, but an individual phenomenon that you carry with you at all times.

REFERENCES

Alderman, Lesley. "How You Can Take Control of Your Career." *Money*, July 1995, p. 37.

Block, Peter. *Flawless Consulting: A Guide to Getting Your Expertise Used.* San Diego, CA: University Associates, 1981.

Carr, Clay. *Teampower: Lessons from America's Top Companies on Putting Teampower to Work.* Englewood Cliffs, NJ: Prentice Hall, 1992.

Carr, Clay. *The Competitive Power of Constant Creativity.* New York, NY: AMACOM, 1994.

Connors, Roger, Tom Smith and Craig Hickman. *The OZ Principle: Getting Results Through Individual and Organizational Accountability.* Englewood Cliffs, NJ: Prentice Hall, 1994.

Covey, Stephen R. *The Seven Habits of Highly Effective People.* New York, NY: Simon and Schuster, 1989.

Dalai Lama. *A Policy of Kindness: An Anthology of Writings by and about the Dalai Lama.* Ithaca, NY: Snow Lion, 1990, pp. 113-14.

Fisher, Roger and William Ury. *Getting to Yes: Negotiating Agreement without Giving In.* Boston, MA: Houghton Mifflin, 1981.

Gardner, Howard. *Leading Minds: An Anatomy of Leadership.* New York, NY: Basic Books, 1995.

Keirsey, David and Marilyn Bates. *Please Understand Me: Character and Temperament Types.* Del Mar, CA: Prometheus Nemesis Book Company, 1984.

Kouzes, James M. and Barry Z. Posner. *The Leadership Challenge: How to Get Extraordinary Things Done in Organizations.* San Francisco, CA: Jossey-Bass, 1987.

Myers, Isabel Briggs, with Peter B. Myers. *Gifts Differing: Understanding Personality Type.* Palo Alto, CA: CPP Books, 1993.

Pfeffer, Jeffrey. *Competitive Advantage Through People: Unleashing the Power of the Workforce.* Boston, MA: Harvard Business School Press, 1994.

Rinpoche, Sogyal. *The Tibetan Book of Living and Dying.* San Francisco, CA: Harper, 1994.

Schoen, Donald A. *The Reflective Practitioner: How Professionals Think in Action.* New York, NY: Basic Books, 1983.

Schrage, Michael. *Shared Minds: The New Technologies of Collaboration.* New York, NY: Doubleday, 1990.

Senge, Peter. *The Fifth Discipline: The Art and Practice of the Learning Organization.* New York, NY: Doubleday, 1990.

Suzuki, Shunryu. *Zen Mind, Beginner's Mind.* New York, NY: Weatherill, 1973.

Thich Nhat Hanh. *Being Peace.* Berkeley, CA: Parallax Press, 1987.

"Trust in Me." *The Economist*, December 16, 1995, p. 61.

"Two Cheers for Loyalty." *The Economist*, January 6, 1996, p. 49.

INDEX